# The Neville Collection

*(Combo of 5 Most Popular Books in a Single Volume)*

# HARDCOVER NON-FICTION

- Abraham Lincoln by Lord Charnwood, ISBN: 9789387669147
- Annihilation of Caste by Dr B.R. Ambedkar, ISBN: 9789390492756
- Be What You Wish by Neville Goddard, ISBN: 9789388118163
- Civilization and Its Discontents by Sigmund Freud, ISBN: 9789388118279
- Guerrilla Warfare by Ernesto Che Guevara, ISBN: 9789391181932
- How I Made 2 Million in the Stock Market by N. Darvas, ISBN: 9789389440218
- Jail Diary and Other Writings by Bhagat Singh, ISBN: 9789390492084
- Man-eaters of Kumaon by Jim Corbett, ISBN: 9789354990038
- My Experiments with Truth by Mahatma Gandhi, ISBN: 9789387669277
- Relativity by Albert Einstein, ISBN: 9789387669185
- Reminiscences of a Stock Operator by Edwin Lefevre, ISBN: 9789390492244
- Scientific Healing Affirmations by P. Yogananda, ISBN: 9789354990137
- The Art of War by Sun Tzu, ISBN: 9789387669321
- The Book of Five Rings by Miyamoto Musashi, ISBN: 9789389440553
- The Diary of a Young Girl by Anne Frank, ISBN: 9789387669208
- The Game of Life and How to Play It by F.S. Shinn, ISBN: 9789388118316
- The Law of Success by Napoleon Hill, ISBN: 9789389157949
- The Origin of Species by Charles Darwin, ISBN: 9789387669345
- The Power of Your Subcon. Mind by Joseph Murphy, ISBN: 9789387669222
- The Psychopathology of Everyday Life by Sigmund Freud, ISBN: 9789388118231
- The Richest Man in Babylon by George S. Clason, ISBN: 9789388118354
- The Science of Getting Rich by Wallace D. Wattles, ISBN: 9789387669239
- The World as I See It by Albert Einstein, ISBN: 9789388118248
- Why I am an Atheist and Other Works by Bhagat Singh, ISBN: 9789354992667
- Zen in the Art of Archery by Eugen Herrigel, ISBN: 9789354990298

**Search the book by its ISBN**

# *The Neville Collection*

*Combo of 5 Most Popular Books in a Single Volume*

NEVILLE GODDARD

GENERAL PRESS

*Published by*
**GENERAL PRESS**
4805/24, Fourth Floor, Krishna House
Ansari Road, Daryaganj, New Delhi - 110002
Ph : 011-23282971, 45795759
E-mail : generalpressindia@gmail.com

**www.generalpress.in**



First Edition : 2023

ISBN : 9789354996245

Published by Azeem Ahmad Khan for General Press

# Contents


**1 *Awakened Imagination* . . . . . . . . . . . . . . . . . . . . . . 9**

1. Who is Your Imagination? . . . . . . . . . . . . . . . . . . . . 11
2. Sealed Instructions . . . . . . . . . . . . . . . . . . . . 18
3. Highways of the Inner World . . . . . . . . . . . . . . . . . . . . 26
4. The Pruning Shears of Revision . . . . . . . . . . . . . . . . . . . . 32
5. The Coin of Heaven . . . . . . . . . . . . . . . . . . . . 39
6. It is Within . . . . . . . . . . . . . . . . . . . . 48
7. Creation is Finished . . . . . . . . . . . . . . . . . . . . 53
8. The Apple of God's Eye . . . . . . . . . . . . . . . . . . . . 60

**2 *Be What You Wish* . . . . . . . . . . . . . . . . . . . . . . 63**

*Introduction* . . . . . . . . . . . . . . . . . . . . 65

1. Be What You Wish . . . . . . . . . . . . . . . . . . . . 67
2. By Imagination We Become . . . . . . . . . . . . . . . . . . . . 72
3. Answered Prayer . . . . . . . . . . . . . . . . . . . . 77
4. Meditation . . . . . . . . . . . . . . . . . . . . 82

5. The Law of Assumption . . . 87
6. Truth . . . 92
7. Stone, Water or Wine? . . . 96
8. Feeling is the Secret . . . 101
9. Affirm the Reality of Our Own Greatness . . . 105

3 ***Feeling is the Secret*** . . . **109**

*Foreword* . . . 111
1. Law and Its Operation . . . 113
2. Sleep . . . 119
3. Prayer . . . 125
4. Spirit – Feeling . . . 128

4 ***The Power of Awareness*** . . . **131**

1. I Am . . . 133
2. Consciousness . . . 136
3. Power of Assumption . . . 138
4. Desire . . . 141
5. The Truth that Sets You Free . . . 143
6. Attention . . . 146
7. Attitude . . . 149
8. Renunciation . . . 153
9. Preparing Your Place . . . 155

10. Creation . . . . . . . . . . 158
11. Interference . . . . . . . . . . 160
12. Subjective Control . . . . . . . . . . 162
13. Acceptance . . . . . . . . . . 164
14. The Effortless Way . . . . . . . . . . 167
15. The Crown of the Mysteries . . . . . . . . . . 169
16. Personal Impotence . . . . . . . . . . 171
17. All Things are Possible . . . . . . . . . . 173
18. Be Ye Doers . . . . . . . . . . 175
19. Essentials . . . . . . . . . . 177
20. Righteousness . . . . . . . . . . 180
21. Free Will . . . . . . . . . . 183
22. Persistence . . . . . . . . . . 186
23. Case Histories . . . . . . . . . . 189
24. Failure . . . . . . . . . . 203
25. Faith . . . . . . . . . . 206
26. Destiny . . . . . . . . . . 209
27. Reverence . . . . . . . . . . 211

5 ***The Secret of Imagining* . . . . . . . . . . 213**

*About the Author* . . . . . . . . . . 232

1

# Awakened Imagination

# 1

# *Who is Your Imagination?*

*I rest not from my great task*
*To open the Eternal Worlds, to open the immortal Eyes*
*Of Man inwards into the Worlds of thought: into Eternity*
*Ever expanding in the Bosom of God, the Human Imagination.*

BLAKE, JERUSALEM 5:18-20

Certain words in the course of long use gather so many strange connotations that they almost cease to mean anything at all. Such a word is imagination. This word is made to serve all manner of ideas, some of them directly opposed to one another. Fancy, thought, hallucination, suspicion: indeed, so wide is its use and so varied its meanings, the word imagination has no status nor fixed significance. For example, we ask a man to "use his imagination", meaning that his present outlook is too restricted and therefore not equal to the task. In the next breath, we tell him that his ideas are "pure imagination", thereby implying that his ideas are unsound. We speak of a jealous or suspicious person as a "victim of his own imagination", meaning that his thoughts are untrue. A minute later we pay a man the highest tribute by describing him as a "man of imagination". Thus the word imagination has no definite meaning. Even the dictionary gives us no help. It defines imagination as: (1) the picturing power or act of the mind, the constructive or creative principle; (2) a phantasm; (3) an irrational notion or belief; (4) planning, plotting or scheming as involving mental construction.

I identify the central figure of the Gospels with human imagination, the power which makes the forgiveness of sins, the achievement of our goals, inevitable.

> *"All things were made by Him; and without him was not anything made that was made."*
>
> **John 1:3**

There is only one thing in the world, Imagination, and all our deformations of it.

> *"He is despised and rejected of men; a man of sorrows, and acquainted with grief."*
>
> **Isaiah 53:3**

Imagination is the very gateway of reality. "Man", said Blake, "is either the ark of God or a phantom of the earth and of the water". "Naturally he is only a natural organ subject to Sense". "The Eternal Body of Man is The Imagination: that is God himself, The Divine Body. Jesus: we are His Members".

I know of no greater and truer definition of the Imagination than that of Blake. By imagination we have the power to be anything we desire to be. Through imagination, we disarm and transform the violence of the world. Our most intimate as well as our most casual relationships become imaginative, as we awaken to "the mystery hid from the ages", that Christ in us is our imagination. We then realize that only as we live by imagination can we truly be said to live at all.

I want this book to be the simplest, clearest, frankest work I have the power to make it, that I may encourage you to function imaginatively, that you may open your "Immortal Eyes inwards into the Worlds of Thought", where you behold every desire of your heart as ripe grain "white already to harvest".

> *"I am come that they might have life, and that they might have it more abundantly."*
>
> **JOHN 10:10**

The abundant life that Christ promised us is ours to experience now, but not until we have the sense of Christ as our imagination can we experience it

> *"The mystery hid from the ages... Christ in you, the hope of glory."*
>
> **COLOSSIANS 1:26, 27**

is your imagination. This is the mystery which I am ever striving to realize more keenly myself and to urge upon others.

Imagination is our redeemer, "the Lord from Heaven" born of man but not begotten of man.

Every man is Mary and birth to Christ must give. If the story of the Immaculate Conception and birth of Christ appears irrational to man, it is only because it is misread as biography, history, and cosmology, and the modern explorers of the imagination do not help by calling It the unconscious or subconscious mind. Imagination's birth and growth is the gradual transition from a God of tradition to a God of experience. If the birth of Christ (imagination) in man seems slow, it is only because man is unwilling to let go the comfortable but false anchorage of tradition.

When imagination is discovered as the first principle of religion, the stone of literal understanding will have felt the rod of Moses and, like the rock of Zin, issue forth the water of psychological meaning to quench the thirst of humanity; and all who take the proffered cup and live a life according to this truth will transform the water of psychological meaning into the wine of forgiveness. Then, like the good Samaritan, they will pour it on the wounds of all.

The Son of God is not to be found in history, nor in any external form. He can only be found as the imagination of him in whom His presence becomes manifest.

> *O, would thy heart but be a manger for His birth! God would once more become a child on earth.*

Man is the garden in which this only-begotten Son of God sleeps. He awakens this Son by lifting his imagination up to heaven and clothing men in godlike stature. We must go on imagining better than the best we know.

Man in the moment of his awakening to the imaginative life must meet the test of Sonship.

> *"Father, reveal Thy Son in me"*
> *and*
> *"It pleased God to reveal His Son in me".*

GALATIANS 1:15, 16

The supreme test of Sonship is the forgiveness of sin. The test that your imagination is Christ Jesus, the Son of God, is your ability to forgive sin. Sin means missing one's mark in life, falling short of one's ideal, failing to achieve one's aim. Forgiveness means identification of man with his ideal or aim in life. This is the work of awakened imagination, the supreme work, for it tests man's ability to enter into and partake of the nature of his opposite.

> *"Let the weak man say, I am strong."*

JOEL 3:10

Reasonably, this is impossible. Only awakened imagination can enter into and partake of the nature of its opposite.

This conception of Christ Jesus as human imagination raises these fundamental questions: Is imagination a power sufficient, not merely to enable me to assume that I am strong, but is it also of itself capable of executing the idea? Suppose that I desire to be in some other place or situation. Could I, by imagining myself into such a state and place, bring about their physical realization? Suppose I could not afford the journey and suppose my present social and financial status oppose the idea that I want to realize. Would imagination be sufficient of itself to incarnate these desires? Does imagination comprehend reason? By reason, I mean deductions from the observations of the senses. Does it recognize the external world of facts? In the practical way of everyday life is imagination a complete guide to behaviour? Suppose I am capable of acting with continuous imagination, that is, suppose I am capable of sustaining the feeling of my wish fulfilled, will my assumption harden into fact? And, if it does harden into fact, shall I on reflection find that my actions through the period of incubation have been reasonable? Is my imagination a power sufficient, not merely to assume the feeling of the wish fulfilled, but is it also of itself capable of incarnating the idea? After assuming that I am already what I want to be, must I continually guide myself by reasonable ideas and actions in order to bring about the fulfilment of my assumption?

Experience has convinced me that an assumption, though false, if persisted in, will harden into fact, that continuous imagination is sufficient for all things, and all my reasonable plans and actions will never make up for my lack of continuous imagination.

Is it not true that the teachings of the Gospels can only be received in terms of faith and that the Son of God is constantly looking for signs of faith in people, that is, faith in their own imagination? Is not the promise

> *"Believe that ye receive and ye shall receive."*
>
> MARK 11:24

the same as "Imagine that you are and you shall be"? Was it not an imaginary state in which Moses

> *"Endured, as seeing Him who is invisible"?*
>
> HEBREWS 11:27

Was it not by the power of his own imagination that he endured?

Truth depends upon the intensity of the imagination, not upon external facts. Facts are the fruit bearing witness of the use or misuse of the imagination. Man becomes what he imagines. He has a self-determined history. Imagination is the way, the truth, the life revealed. We cannot get hold of truth with the logical mind. Where the natural man of sense sees a bud, imagination sees a rose full-blown. Truth cannot be encompassed by facts. As we awaken to the imaginative life, we discover that to imagine a thing is to make it so, that a true judgment need not conform to the external reality to which it relates.

The imaginative man does not deny the reality of the sensuous outer world of Becoming, but he knows that it is the inner world of continuous Imagination that is the force by which the sensuous outer world of Becoming is brought to pass. He sees the outer world and all its happenings as projections of the inner world of Imagination. To him, everything is a manifestation of the mental activity which goes on in man's imagination, without the sensuous reasonable man being aware of it. But he realizes that every man must become conscious of this inner activity and see the relationship between the inner causal world of imagination and the sensuous outer world of effects.

It is a marvelous thing to find that you can imagine yourself into the state of your fulfilled desire and escape from the jails which ignorance built.

The Real Man is a Magnificent Imagination.

It is this self that must be awakened.

> *"Awake thou that sleepest, and arise from the dead, and Christ shall give the light."*
>
> EPHESIANS 5:14

The moment man discovers that his imagination is Christ, he accomplishes acts which on this level can only be called miraculous. But until man has the sense of Christ as his imagination

*"You did not choose me, I have chosen you."*

**John 15:16**

he will see everything in pure objectivity without any subjective relationship. Not realizing that all that he encounters is part of himself, he rebels at the thought that he has chosen the conditions of his life, that they are related by affinity to his own mental activity. Man must firmly come to believe that reality lies within him and not without.

Although others have bodies, a life of their own, their reality is rooted in you, ends in you, as yours ends in God.

## 2

# Sealed Instructions

*The first power that meets us at the threshold of the soul's domain is the power of imagination.*

DR. FRANZ HARTMANN

I was first made conscious of the power, nature, and redemptive function of imagination through the teachings of my friend Abdullah; and through subsequent experiences, I learned that Jesus was a symbol of the coming of imagination to man, that the test of His birth in man was the individual's ability to forgive sin; that is, his ability to identify himself or another with his aim in life.

Without the identification of man with his aim, the forgiveness of sin is an impossibility, and only the Son of God can forgive sin. Therefore, man's ability to identify himself with his aim, though reason and his senses deny it, is proof of the birth of Christ in him. To passively surrender to appearances and bow before the evidence of facts is to confess that Christ is not yet born in you.

Although this teaching shocked and repelled me at first, for I was a convinced and earnest Christian, and did not then know that Christianity could not be inherited by the mere accident of birth but must be consciously adopted as a way of life—it stole later on, through visions, mystical revelations, and practical experiences, into my understanding and found its interpretation in a deeper mood. But I must confess that it is a trying time when those things are shaken which one has always taken for granted.

> *"Seest thou these great buildings? There shall not be left one stone upon another that shall not be thrown down."*
>
> **MARK 13:2**

Not one stone of literal understanding will be left after one drinks the water of psychological meaning. All that has been built up by natural religion is cast into the flames of mental fire. Yet, what better way is there to understand Christ Jesus than to identify the central character of the Gospels with human imagination, knowing that, every time you exercise your imagination lovingly on behalf of another, you are literally mediating God to man and thereby feeding and clothing Christ Jesus and that, whenever you imagine evil against another, you are literally beating and crucifying Christ Jesus? Every imagination of man is either the cup of cold water or the sponge of vinegar to the parched lips of Christ.

> *Let none of you imagine evil in your hearts against his neighbour*

warned the prophet Zechariah. When man heeds this advice, he will awake from the imposed sleep of Adam into the full consciousness of the Son of God. He is in the world, and the world is made by Him, and the world knows Him not: Human Imagination.

I asked myself many times, "If my imagination is Christ Jesus and all things are possible to Christ Jesus, are all things possible to me?"

Through experience, I have come to know that, when I identify myself with my aim in life, then Christ is awake in me.

Christ is sufficient for all things.

> *"I lay down my life that I might take it again. No man taketh it from me, but I lay it down of myself."*
>
> **JOHN 10:17, 18**

What a comfort it is to know that all that I experience is the result of my own standard of beliefs; that I am the center of my own web of circumstances and that as I change, so must my outer world!

The world presents different appearances according as our states of consciousness differ. What we see when we are identified with a state cannot be seen when we are no longer fused with it. By state is meant all that man believes and consents to as true. No idea presented to the mind can realize itself unless the mind accepts it. It depends on the acceptance, the state with which we are identified, how things present themselves. In the fusion of imagination and states is to be found the shaping of the world as it seems. The world is a revelation of the states with which imagination is fused. It is the state from which we think that determines the objective world in which we live. The rich man, the poor man, the good man, the thief are what they are by virtue of the states from which they view the world. On the distinction between these states depends the distinction between the worlds of these men. Individually so different is this same world. It is not the actions and behaviour of the good man that should be matched but his point of view. Outer reforms are useless if the inner state is not changed. Success is gained not by imitating the outer actions of the successful but by right inner actions and inner talking.

If we detach ourselves from a state, and we may at any moment, the conditions and circumstances to which that union gave being vanish.

It was in the fall of 1933 in New York City that I approached Abdullah with a problem. He asked me one simple question, "What do you want?" I told him that I would like to spend the winter in Barbados, but that I was broke. I literally did not have a nickel.

"If you will imagine yourself to be in Barbados", said he, "thinking and viewing the world from that state of consciousness instead of thinking of Barbados, you will spend the winter there." "You must not concern yourself with the ways and means of getting there, for the state of consciousness of already being in Barbados, if occupied by your imagination, will devise the means best suited to realize itself."

Man lives by committing himself to invisible states, by fusing his imagination with what he knows to be other than himself, and in this union he experiences the results of that fusion. No one can lose what he has, save by detachment from the state where the things experienced have their natural life.

"You must imagine yourself right into the state of your fulfilled desire", Abdullah told me, "and fall asleep viewing the world from Barbados."

The world which we describe from observation must be as we describe it relative to ourselves. Our imagination connects us with the state desired. But we must use imagination masterfully, not as an onlooker thinking of the end, but as a partaker thinking from the end. We must actually be there in imagination. If we do this, our subjective experience will be realized objectively.

"This is not mere fancy", said he, "but a truth you can prove by experience."

His appeal to enter into the wish fulfilled was the secret of thinking from the end. Every state is already there as "mere possibility" as long as you think of it, but is overpoweringly real when you think from it. Thinking from the end is the way of Christ.

I began right there and then, fixing my thoughts beyond the limits of sense, beyond that aspect to which my present state gave being, towards the feeling of already being in Barbados and viewing the world from that standpoint.

He emphasized the importance of the state from which man views the world as he falls asleep. All prophets claim that the voice of God is chiefly heard by man in dreams.

> *"In a dream, in a vision of the night, when deep sleep falleth upon men, in slumbering upon the bed; then he openeth the ears of men, and sealeth their instruction."*
>
> JOB 33:15, 16

That night and for several nights thereafter, I fell asleep in the assumption that I was in my father's house in Barbados. Within a month, I received a letter from my brother, saying that he had a strong desire to have the family together at Christmas and asking me to use the enclosed steamship ticket for Barbados. I sailed two days after I received my brother's letter and spent a wonderful winter in Barbados.

This experience has convinced me that man can be anything he pleases if he will make the conception habitual and think from the end. It has also shown me that I can no longer excuse myself by placing the blame on the world of external things, that my good and my evil have no dependency except from myself, that it depends on the state from which I view the world how things present themselves.

Man, who is free in his choice, acts from conceptions which he freely, though not always wisely, chooses. All conceivable states are awaiting our choice and occupancy, but no amount of rationalizing will of itself yield us the state of consciousness which is the only thing worth having.

The imaginative image is the only thing to seek.

The ultimate purpose of imagination is to create in us "the spirit of Jesus", which is continual forgiveness of sin, continual identification of man with his ideal. Only by identifying ourselves with our aim can we forgive ourselves for having missed it. All else is labor in vain. On this path, to whatever place or state we convey our imagination, to that place or state we will gravitate physically also.

> *"In my Father's house are many mansions; if it were not so, I would have told you. I go to prepare a place for you. And if I go and prepare a place for you, I will come again, and receive you unto myself; that where I am, there ye may be also."*
>
> JOHN 14:2, 3

By sleeping in my father's house in my imagination as though I slept there in the flesh, I used my imagination with that state and was compelled to experience that state in the flesh also.

So vivid was this state to me, I could have been seen in my father's house had any sensitive entered the room where in imagination I was sleeping. A man can be seen where in imagination he is, for a man must be where his imagination is, for his imagination is himself. This I know from experience, for I have been seen by a few to whom I desired to be seen, when physically I was hundreds of miles away.

I, by the intensity of my imagination and feeling, imagining and feeling myself to be in Barbados instead of merely thinking of Barbados, had spanned the vast Atlantic to influence my brother into desiring my presence to complete the family circle at Christmas. Thinking from the end, from the feeling of my wish fulfilled, was the source of everything that happened as outer cause, such as my brother's impulse to send me a steamship ticket; and it was also the cause of everything that appeared as results.

In Ideas of Good and Evil, W. B. Yeats, having described a few experiences similar to this experience of mine, writes:

> *If all who have described events like this have not dreamed, we should rewrite our histories, for all men, certainly all imaginative men, must be forever casting forth enchantments, glamour, illusions; and all men, especially tranquil men who have no powerful egotistic life, must be continually passing under their power.*

Determined imagination, thinking from the end, is the beginning of all miracles.

I would like to give you an immense belief in miracles, but a miracle is only the name given by those who have no knowledge of the power and function of imagination to the works of imagination. Imagining oneself into the feeling of the wish fulfilled is the means by which a new state is entered. This gives the state the quality of is-ness. Hermes tells us:

> *That which is, is manifested; that which has been or shall be, is un-manifested, but not dead; for Soul, the eternal activity of God, animates all things.*

The future must become the present in the imagination of the one who would wisely and consciously create circumstances. We must translate vision into Being, thinking of into thinking from. Imagination must center itself in some state and view the world from that state. Thinking from the end is an intense perception of the world of fulfilled desire. Thinking from the state desired is creative living. Ignorance of this ability to think from the end is bondage. It is the root of all bondage with which man is bound. To passively surrender to the evidence of the senses underestimates the capacities of the Inner Self. Once man accepts thinking from the end as a creative principle in which he can cooperate, then he is redeemed from the absurdity of ever attempting to achieve his objective by merely thinking of it.

Construct all ends according to the pattern of fulfilled desire.

The whole of life is just the appeasement of hunger, and the infinite states of consciousness from which a man can view the world are purely a means of satisfying that hunger. The principle upon which each state is organized is some form of hunger to lift the passion for self-gratification to ever higher and higher levels of experience. Desire is the mainspring of the mental machinery. It is a blessed thing. It is a right and natural craving which has a state of consciousness as its right and natural satisfaction.

> *"But one thing I do, forgetting the things which are behind, and stretching forward to the things which are before, I press on toward the goal."*
>
> **PHILIPPIANS 3:13, 14**

It is necessary to have an aim in life. Without an aim, we drift. "What wantest thou of me?" is the implied question asked most often by the central figure of the Gospels. In defining your aim, you must want it.

> *"As the hart panteth after the water brooks, so panteth my soul after Thee, O, God."*
>
> **PSALMS 42:1**

It is lack of this passionate direction to life that makes man fail of accomplishment.

The spanning of the bridge between desire, thinking of, and satisfaction, thinking from, is all-important. We must move mentally from thinking of the end to thinking from the end. This, reason could never do. By its nature, it is restricted to the evidence of the senses; but imagination, having no such limitation, can. Desire exists to be gratified in the activity of imagination. Through imagination, man escapes from the limitation of the senses and the bondage of reason.

There is no stopping the man who can think from the end. Nothing can stop him. He creates the means and grows his way out of limitation into ever greater and greater mansions of the Lord. It does not matter what he has been or what he is. All that matters is "what does he want?" He knows that the world is a manifestation of the mental activity which goes on within himself, so he strives to determine and control the ends from which he thinks. In his imagination he dwells in the end, confident that he shall dwell there in the flesh also. He puts his whole trust in the feeling of the wish fulfilled and lives by committing himself to that state, for the art of fortune is to tempt him so to do. Like the man at the pool of Bethesda, he is ready for the moving of the waters of imagination. Knowing that every desire is ripe grain to him who knows how to think from the end, he is indifferent to mere reasonable probability and confident that through continuous imagination his assumptions will harden into fact.

But how to persuade men everywhere that thinking from the end is the only living, how to foster it in every activity of man, how to reveal it as the plenitude of life and not the compensation of the disappointed: that is the problem.

Life is a controllable thing. You can experience what you please once you realize that you are His Son, and that you are what you are by virtue of the state of consciousness from which you think and view the world,

*"Son, thou art ever with me, and all that I have is thine."*

LUKE 15:31

# 3

# *Highways of the Inner World*

> *"And the children struggled within her... and the Lord said unto her, two nations are in thy womb, and two manner of people shall be separated from thy bowels; and the one people shall be stronger than the other people; and the elder shall serve the younger."*
>
> GENESIS 25:22-23

Duality is an inherent condition of life. Everything that exists is double. Man is a dual creature with contrary principles embedded in his nature. They war within him and present attitudes to life which are antagonistic. This conflict is the eternal enterprise, the war in heaven, the never ending struggle of the younger or inner man of imagination to assert His supremacy over the elder or outer man of sense.

> *"The first shall be last and the last shall be first."*
>
> MATTHEW 19:30

> *"He it is, who coming after me is preferred before me."*
>
> JOHN 1:27

> *"The second man is the Lord from heaven."*
>
> 1 COR. 15:47

Man begins to awake to the imaginative life the moment he feels the presence of another being in himself.

> *"In your limbs lie nations twain, rival races from their birth; one the mastery shall gain, the younger o'er the elder reign."*

There are two distinct centers of thought or outlooks on the world possessed by every man. The Bible speaks of these two outlooks as natural and spiritual.

> *"The natural man receiveth not the things of the Spirit of God: for they are foolishness unto him: neither can he know them, because they are spiritually discerned."*
>
> I CORINTHIANS 2:14

Man's inner body is as real in the world of subjective experience as his outer physical body is real in the world of external realities, but the inner body expresses a more fundamental part of reality. This existing inner body of man must be consciously exercised and directed. The inner world of thought and feeling to which the inner body is attuned has its real structure and exists in its own higher space.

There are two kinds of movement, one that is according to the inner body and another that is according to the outer body. The movement which is according to the inner body is causal, but the outer movement is under compulsion. The inner movement determines the outer which is joined to it, bringing into the outer a movement that is similar to the actions of the inner body. Inner movement is the force by which all events are brought to pass. Outer movement is subject to the compulsion applied to it by the movement of the inner body.

Whenever the actions of the inner body match the actions which the outer must take to appease desire, that desire will be realized.

Construct mentally a drama which implies that your desire is realized and make it one which involves movement of self. Immobilize your outer physical self. Act precisely as though you were going to take a nap, and start the predetermined action in imagination. A vivid representation of the action is the beginning of that action. Then, as you are falling asleep, consciously imagine yourself into the scene. The length of the sleep is not important, a short nap is sufficient, but carrying the action into sleep thickens fancy into fact.

At first your thoughts may be like rambling sheep that have no shepherd. Don't despair. Should your attention stray seventy times seven, bring it back seventy times seven to its predetermined course until from sheer exhaustion it follows the appointed path. The inner journey must never be without direction. When you take to the inner road, it is to do what you did mentally before you started. You go for the prize you have already seen and accepted.

In The Road to Xanadu, Professor John Livingston Lowes says:

> *"But I have long had the feeling, which this study had matured to a conviction, that Fancy and Imagination are not two powers at all, but one. The valid distinction which exists between them lies, not in the materials with which they operate, but in the degree of intensity of the operant power itself. Working at high tension, the imaginative energy assimilates and transmutes; keyed low, the same energy aggregates and yokes together those images which at its highest pitch, it merges indissolubly into one."*

Fancy assembles, imagination fuses.

Here is a practical application of this theory. A year ago, a blind girl living in the city of San Francisco found herself confronted with a transportation problem. A rerouting of buses forced her to make three transfers between her home and her office. This lengthened her trip from fifteen minutes to two hours and fifteen minutes. She thought seriously about this problem and came to the decision that a car was the solution. She knew that she could not drive a car but felt that she could be driven in one. Putting this theory to the test that "whenever the actions of the inner self correspond to the actions which the outer, physical self must take to appease desire, that desire will be realized", she said to herself, "I will sit here and imagine that I am being driven to my office."

Sitting in her living room, she began to imagine herself seated in a car. She felt the rhythm of the motor. She imagined that she smelled the odor of gasoline, felt the motion of the car, touched the sleeve of the driver and felt that the driver was a man. She felt the car stop, and turning to her companion, said, "Thank you very much, sir." To which he replied, "The pleasure is all mine." Then she stepped from the car and heard the door snap shut as she closed it.

She told me that she centered her imagination on being in a car and, although blind, viewed the city from her imaginary ride. She did not think of the ride. She thought from the ride and all that it implied. This controlled and subjectively directed purposive ride raised her imagination to its full potency. She kept her purpose ever before her, knowing there was cohesion in purposive inner movement. In these mental journeys, an emotional continuity must be sustained, the emotion of fulfilled desire. Expectancy and desire were so intensely joined that they passed at once from a mental state into a physical act.

The inner self moves along the predetermined course best when the emotions collaborate. The inner self must be fired, and it is best fired by the thought of great deeds and personal gain. We must take pleasure in our actions.

On two successive days, the blind girl took her imaginary ride, giving it all the joy and sensory vividness of reality. A few hours after her second imaginary ride, a friend told her of a story in the evening paper. It was a story of a man who was interested in the blind. The blind girl phoned him and stated her problem. The very next day, on his way home, he stopped in at a bar and while there had the urge to tell the story of the blind girl to his friend the proprietor. A total stranger, on hearing the story, volunteered to drive the blind girl home every day. The man who told the story then said, "If you will take her home, I will take her to work."

This was over a year ago, and since that day, this blind girl has been driven to and from her office by these two gentlemen. Now, instead of spending two hours and fifteen minutes on three buses, she is at her office in less than fifteen minutes. And on that first ride to her office, she turned to her good Samaritan and said, "Thank you very much, sir"; and he replied, "The pleasure is all mine."

Thus, the objects of her imagination were to her the realities of which the physical manifestation was only the witness. The determinative animating principle was the imaginative ride. Her triumph could be a surprise only to those who did not know of her inner ride. She mentally viewed the world from this imaginative ride with such a clearness of vision that every aspect of the city attained identity. These inner movements not only produce corresponding outer movements: this is the law which operates beneath all physical appearances. He who practices these exercises of bilocation will develop unusual powers of concentration and quiescence and will inevitably achieve waking consciousness on the inner and dimensionally larger world. Actualizing strongly, she fulfilled her desire, for, viewing the city from the feeling of her wish fulfilled, she matched the state desired and granted that to herself which sleeping men ask of God.

To realize your desire, an action must start in your imagination, apart from the evidence of the senses, involving movement of self and implying fulfilment of your desire. Whenever it is the action which the outer self takes to appease desire, that desire will be realized.

The movement of every visible object is caused not by things outside the body, but by things within it, which operate from within outward. The journey is in yourself. You travel along the highways of the inner world. Without inner movement, it is impossible to bring forth anything. Inner action is introverted sensation. If you will construct mentally a drama which implies that you have realized your objective, then close your eyes and drop your thoughts inward, centering your imagination all the while in the predetermined action and partake in that action, you will become a self-determined being.

Inner action orders all things according to the nature of itself. Try it and see whether a desirable ideal once formulated is possible, for only by this process of experiment can you realize your potentialities. It is thus that this creative principle is being realized. So the clue to purposive living is to center your imagination in the action and feeling of fulfilled desire with such awareness, such sensitiveness, that you initiate and experience movement upon the inner world.

Ideas only act if they are felt, if they awaken inner movement. Inner movement is conditioned by self-motivation, outer movement by compulsion.

> *"Wherever the sole of your foot shall tread, the same give I unto you."*
>
> JOSHUA 1:3

and remember,

> *"The Lord thy God in the midst of thee is mighty."*
>
> ZEPHANIAH 3:17

4

# *The Pruning Shears of Revision*

*"The second Man is the Lord from Heaven."*

1 CORINTHIANS 15:47

*Never will he say caterpillars. He'll say, "There's a lot of butter-flies-as-is-to-be on our cabbages, Prue." He won't say, "It's winter." He'll say, "Summer's sleeping."And there's no bud little enough nor sad-colored enough for Kester not to callen it the beginnings of the blow.*

MARY WEBB, PRECIOUS BANE

The very first act of correction or cure is always "revise". One must start with oneself. It is one's attitude that must be changed.

*What we are, that only can we see.*

EMERSON

It is a most healthy and productive exercise to daily relive the day as you wish you had lived it, revising the scenes to make them conform to your ideals. For instance, suppose today's mail brought disappointing news. Revise the letter. Mentally rewrite it and make it conform to the news you wish you had received. Then, in imagination, read the revised letter over and over again. This is the essence of revision, and revision results in repeal.

The one requisite is to arouse your attention in a way and to such intensity that you become wholly absorbed in the revised action. You will experience an expansion and refinement of the senses by this imaginative exercise and eventually achieve vision. But always remember that the ultimate purpose of this exercise is to create in you "the Spirit of Jesus", which is continual forgiveness of sin.

Revision is of greatest importance when the motive is to change oneself, when there is a sincere desire to be something different, when the longing is to awaken the ideal active spirit of forgiveness. Without imagination, man remains a being of sin. Man either goes forward to imagination or remains imprisoned in his senses. To go forward to imagination is to forgive. Forgiveness is the life of the imagination. The art of living is the art of forgiving. Forgiveness is, in fact, experiencing in imagination the revised version of the day, experiencing in imagination what you wish you had experienced in the flesh. Every time one really forgives, that is, every time one relives the event as it should have been lived, one is born again.

"Father, forgive them" is not the plea that comes once a year but the opportunity that comes every day. The idea of forgiving is a daily possibility, and, if it is sincerely done, it will lift man to higher and higher levels of being. He will experience a daily Easter, and Easter is the idea of rising transformed. And that should be almost a continuous process.

Freedom and forgiveness are indissolubly linked. Not to forgive is to be at war with ourselves, for we are freed according to our capacity to forgive.

> *"Forgive, and you shall be forgiven."*
>
> **Luke 6:37**

Forgive, not merely from a sense of duty or service; forgive because you want to.

> *"Thy ways are ways of pleasantness and all thy paths are peace."*
>
> PROVERBS 3:17

You must take pleasure in revision. You can forgive others effectively only when you have a sincere desire to identify them with their ideal. Duty has no momentum. Forgiveness is a matter of deliberately withdrawing attention from the unrevised day and giving it full strength, and joyously, to the revised day. If a man begins to revise even a little of the vexations and troubles of the day, then he begins to work practically on himself. Every revision is a victory over himself and therefore a victory over his enemy

> *"A man's foes are those of his own household."*
>
> MATTHEW 10:36

and his household is his state of mind. He changes his future as he revises his day.

When a man practices the art of forgiveness, of revision, however factual the scene on which sight then rests, he revises it with his imagination and gazes on one never before witnessed. The magnitude of the change which any act of revision involves makes such change appear wholly improbable to the realist, the unimaginative man; but the radical changes in the fortunes of the Prodigal were all produced by a "change of heart".

The battle man fights is fought out in his own imagination. The man who does not revise the day has lost the vision of that life, into the likeness of which it is the true labor of the "Spirit of Jesus" to transform this life.

> *"All things whatsoever ye would that men should do to you, even so do ye to them: for this is the law."*
>
> MATTHEW 7:12

Here is the way an artist friend forgave herself and was set free from pain, annoyance and unfriendliness. Knowing that nothing but forgetfulness and forgiveness will bring us to new values, she cast herself upon her imagination and escaped from the prison of her senses. She writes:

"Thursday, I taught all day in the art school. Only one small thing marred the day. Coming into my afternoon classroom, I discovered the janitor had left all the chairs on top of the desks after cleaning the floor. As I lifted a chair down, it slipped from my grasp and struck me a sharp blow on the instep of my right foot. I immediately examined my thoughts and found that I had criticized the man for not doing his job properly. Since he had lost his helper, I realized he probably felt he had done more than enough and it was an unwanted gift that had bounced and hit me on the foot. Looking down at my foot, I saw both my skin and nylons were intact, so forgot the whole thing.

"That night, after I had been working intensely for about three hours on a drawing, I decided to make myself a cup of coffee. To my utter amazement, I couldn't manage my right foot at all and it was giving out great bumps of pain. I hopped over to a chair and took off my slipper to look at it. The entire foot was a strange purplish pink, swollen out of shape and red hot. I tried walking on it and found that it just flapped. I had no control over it whatsoever. It looked like one of two things: either I had cracked a bone when I dropped the chair on it or something could be dislocated.

"'No use speculating what it is. Better get rid of it right away.' So I became quiet, all ready to melt myself into light. To my complete bewilderment, my imagination refused to cooperate. It just said 'No.' This sort of thing often happens when I am painting. I just started to argue 'Why not?' It just kept saying 'No.' Finally, I gave up and said, 'You know I am in pain. I am trying hard not to be frightened, but you are the boss. What do you want to do?' The answer: 'Go to bed and review the day's events.' So I said 'All right. But let me tell you if my foot isn't perfect by tomorrow morning, you have only yourself to blame.'

"After arranging the bed clothes so they didn't touch my foot, I started to review the day. It was slow going as I had difficulty keeping my attention away from my foot. I went through the whole day, saw nothing to add to the chair incident. But when I reached the early evening, I found myself coming face to face with a man who for the past year has made a point of not speaking. The first time this happened, I thought he had grown deaf. I had known him since school days, but we had never done more than say 'hello' and comment on the weather. Mutual friends assured me I had done nothing, that he had said he never liked me and finally decided it was not worthwhile speaking. I had said 'Hi!' "He hadn't answered. I found that I thought 'Poor guy—what a horrid state to be in. I shall do something about this ridiculous state of affairs.' So, in my imagination, I stopped right there and re-did the scene. I said 'Hi!' He answered 'Hi!' and smiled. I now thought 'Good old Ex.'s ran the scene over a couple of times and went on to the next incident and finished up the day.

"'Now what—do we do my foot or the concert?' I had been melting and wrapping up a wonderful present of courage and success for a friend who was to make her debut the following day and I had been looking forward to giving it to her tonight. My imagination sounded a little bit solemn as it said 'Let us do the concert. It will be more fun.' But first couldn't we just take my perfectly good imagination foot out of this physical one before we start?' I pleaded. 'By all means.'

"That done, I had a lovely time at the concert and my friend got a tremendous ovation.

"By now I was very, very sleepy and fell asleep doing my project. The next morning, as I was putting on my slipper, I suddenly had a quick memory picture of withdrawing a discolored and swollen foot from the same slipper. I took my foot out and looked at it. It was perfectly normal in every respect. There was a tiny pink spot on the instep where I remembered I had hit it with the chair.' What a vivid dream that was!' I thought and dressed. "While waiting for my coffee, I wandered over to my drafting table and saw that all my brushes were lying helter-skelter and unwashed. 'Whatever possessed you to leave your brushes like that?"Don't you remember? It was because of your foot.' So it hadn't been a dream after all, but a beautiful healing."

She had won by the art of revision what she would never have won by force.

> *In Heaven, the only Art of Living Is Forgetting & Forgiving. Especially to the Female.*
>
> BLAKE

We should take our life, not as it appears to be, but from the vision of this artist, from the vision of the world made perfect that is buried under all minds—buried and waiting for us to revise the day.

> *We are led to believe a lie when we see with, not through the eye.*
>
> BLAKE

A revision of the day, and what she held to be so stubbornly real was no longer so to her and, like a dream, had quietly faded away.

You can revise the day to please yourself and by experiencing in imagination the revised speech and actions not only modify the trend of your life story but turn all its discords into harmonies. The one who discovers the secret of revision cannot do otherwise than let himself be guided by love. Your effectiveness will increase with practice. Revision is the way by which right can find its appropriate might. "Resist not evil", for all passionate conflicts result in an interchange of characteristics.

> *"To him that knoweth to do good, and doeth it not, to him it is sin."*
>
> JAMES 4:17

To know the truth, you must live the truth, and to live the truth, your inner actions must match the actions of your fulfilled desire. Expectancy and desire must become one. Your outer world is only actualized inner movement. Through ignorance of the law of revision, those who take to warfare are perpetually defeated.

Only concepts that idealize, depict the truth.

Your ideal of man is his truest self. It is because I firmly believe that whatever is most profoundly imaginative is, in reality, most directly practical that I ask you to live imaginatively and to think into, and to personally appropriate the transcendent saying "Christ in you, the hope of glory."

Don't blame; only resolve. It is not man and the earth at their loveliest, but you practicing the art of revision make paradise. The evidence of this truth can lie only in your own experience of it. Try revising the day. It is to the pruning shears of revision that we owe our prime fruit.

# 5

# The Coin of Heaven

*"Does a firm persuasion that a thing is so, make it so?" And the prophet replied, "All poets believe that it does. And in ages of imagination, this firm persuasion removed mountains: but many are not capable of a firm persuasion of anything."*

BLAKE, MARRIAGE OF HEAVEN AND HELL

*"Let every man be fully persuaded in his own mind."*

ROMANS 14:5

Persuasion is an inner effort of intense attention. To listen attentively as though you heard is to evoke, to activate. By listening, you can hear what you want to hear and persuade those beyond the range of the outer ear. Speak it inwardly in your imagination only. Make your inner conversation match your fulfilled desire. What you desire to hear without, you must hear within. Embrace the without within and become one who hears only that which implies the fulfilment of his desire, and all the external happenings in the world will become a bridge leading to the objective realization of your desire.

Your inner speech is perpetually written all around you in happenings. Learn to relate these happenings to your inner speech and you will become self-taught. By inner speech is meant those mental conversations which you carry on with yourself. They may be inaudible when you are awake because of the noise and distractions of the outer world of becoming, but they are quite audible in deep meditation and dream. But whether they be audible or inaudible, you are their author and fashion your world in their likeness."

> *There is a God in heaven [and heaven is within you] that revealeth secrets, and maketh known to the king Nebuchadnezzar what shall be in the latter days. Thy dream, and the visions of thy head upon thy bed, are these."*
>
> **Daniel 2:28**

Inner speech from premises of fulfilled desire is the way to create an intelligible world for yourself. Observe your inner speech for it is the cause of future action. Inner speech reveals the state of consciousness from which you view the world. Make your inner speech match your fulfilled desire, for your inner speech is manifested all around you in happenings.

> *"If any man offend not in word, the same is a perfect man and able also to bridle the whole body. Behold, we put bits in the horses' mouths, that they may obey us; and we turn about their whole body. Behold also the ships, which though they be so great, and are driven by fierce winds, yet are they turned about with a very small helm, whithersoever the governor listeth. Even so the tongue is a little member, and boasteth great things. Behold, how great a matter a little fire kindleth!"*
>
> **James 3:2-5**

The whole manifested world goes to show us what use we have made of the Word—Inner Speech. An uncritical observation of our inner talking will reveal to us the ideas from which we view the world. Inner talking mirrors our imagination, and our imagination mirrors the state with which it is fused. If the state with which we are fused is the cause of the phenomenon of our life, then we are relieved of the burden of wondering what to do, for we have no alternative but to identify ourselves with our aim, and inasmuch as the state with which we are identified mirrors itself in our inner speech, then to change the state with which we are fused, we must first change our inner talking. It is our inner conversations which make tomorrow's facts.

> *"Put off the former conversation, the old man, which is corrupt... and be renewed in the spirit of your mind... put on the new man, which is created in righteousness."*
>
> EPHESIANS 4:22-24

> *Our minds, like our stomachs, are whetted by change of food.*
>
> QUINTILLIAN

Stop all of the old mechanical negative inner talking and start a new positive and constructive inner speech from premises of fulfilled desire. Inner talking is the beginning, the sowing of the seeds of future action. To determine the action, you must consciously initiate and control your inner talking. Construct a sentence which implies the fulfilment of your aim, such as "I have a large, steady, dependable income, consistent with integrity and mutual benefit", or "I am happily married", "I am wanted", "I am contributing to the good of the world", and repeat such a sentence over and over until you are inwardly affected by it. Our inner speech represents in various ways the world we live in.

> *"In the beginning was the Word."*
>
> JOHN 1:1

> *That which ye sow ye reap. See yonder fields! The sesamum was sesamum, the corn was corn. The Silence and the Darkness knew! So is a man's fate born.*
>
> THE LIGHT OF ASIA

Ends run true to origins.

> *Those that go searching for love only make manifest their own lovelessness. And the loveless never find love, only the loving find love, and they never have to seek for it.*
>
> D. H. Lawrence

Man attracts what he is. The art of life is to sustain the feeling of the wish fulfilled and let things come to you, not to go after them or think they flee away.

Observe your inner talking and remember your aim. Do they match? Does your inner talking match what you would say audibly had you achieved your goal? The individual's inner speech and actions attract the conditions of his life. Through uncritical self-observation of your inner talking you find where you are in the inner world, and where you are in the inner world is what you are in the outer world. You put on the new man whenever ideals and inner speech match. In this way alone can the new man be born.

Inner talking matures in the dark. From the dark it issues into the light. The right inner speech is the speech that would be yours were you to realize your ideal. In other words, it is the speech of fulfilled desire.

"I am that."

> *There are two gifts which God has bestowed upon man alone, and on no other mortal creature. These two are mind and speech; and the gift of mind and speech is equivalent to that of immortality. If a man uses these two gifts rightly, he will differ in nothing from the immortals... and when he quits the body, mind and speech will be his guides, and by them he will be brought into the troop of the gods and the souls that have attained to bliss.*
>
> Hermetica, Walter Scott's translation

The circumstances and conditions of life are out pictured inner talking, solidified sound. Inner speech calls events into existence. In every event, is the creative sound that is its life and being. All that a man believes and consents to as true reveals itself in his inner speech. It is his Word, his life.

Try to notice what you are saying in yourself at this moment, to what thoughts and feelings you are consenting. They will be perfectly woven into your tapestry of life. To change your life, you must change your inner talking, for "life", said Hermes, "is the union of Word and Mind". When imagination matches your inner speech to fulfilled desire, there will then be a straight path in yourself from within out, and the without will instantly reflect the within for you, and you will know reality is only actualized inner talking.

> *"Receive with meekness the inborn word which is able to save your souls."*
>
> JAMES 1:21

Every stage of man's progress is made by the conscious exercise of his imagination matching his inner speech to his fulfilled desire. Because man does not perfectly match them, the results are uncertain, while they might be perfectly certain. Persistent assumption of the wish fulfilled is the means of fulfilling the intention. As we control our inner talking, matching it to our fulfilled desires, we can lay aside all other processes. Then we simply act by clear imagination and intention. We imagine the wish fulfilled and carry on mental conversations from that premise.

Through controlled inner talking from premises of fulfilled desire, seeming miracles are performed. The future becomes the present and reveals itself in our inner speech. To be held by the inner speech of fulfilled desire is to be safely anchored in life. Our lives may seem to be broken by events, but they are never broken so long as we retain the inner speech of fulfilled desire. All happiness depends on the active voluntary use of imagination to construct and inwardly affirm that we are what we want to be. We match ourselves to our ideals by constantly remembering our aim and identifying ourselves with it. We fuse with our aims by frequently occupying the feeling of our wish fulfilled. It is the frequency, the habitual occupancy, that is the secret of success. The oftener we do it, the more natural it is. Fancy assembles. Continuous imagination fuses.

It is possible to resolve every situation by the proper use of imagination. Our task is to get the right sentence, the one which implies that our desire is realized, and fire the imagination with it. All this is intimately connected with the mystery of "the still small voice".

Inner talking reveals the activities of imagination, activities which are the causes of the circumstances of life. As a rule, man is totally unaware of his inner talking and therefore sees himself not as the cause but the victim of circumstance. To consciously create circumstance, man must consciously direct his inner speech, matching "the still small voice" to his fulfilled desires.

> *"He calls things not seen as though they were."*
>
> **ROMANS 4:17**

Right inner speech is essential. It is the greatest of the arts. It is the way out of limitation into freedom. Ignorance of this art has made the world a battlefield and penitentiary where blood and sweat alone are expected, when it should be a place of marveling and wondering. Right inner talking is the first step to becoming what you want to be.

> *Speech is an image of mind, and mind is an image of God.*
>
> **HERMETICA, SCOTT TRANSLATION**

On the morning of April 12, 1953, my wife was awakened by the sound of a great voice of authority speaking within her and saying, "You must stop spending your thoughts, time, and money. Everything in life must be an investment."

To spend is to waste, to squander, to layout without return. To invest is to layout for a purpose from which a profit is expected. This revelation of my wife is about the importance of the moment. It is about the transformation of the moment. What we desire does not lie in the future but in ourselves at this very moment. At any moment in our lives, we are faced with an infinite choice: "what we are and what we want to be". And what we want to be is already existent, but to realize it we must match our inner speech and actions to it.

> *"If two of you shall agree on earth as touching anything that they shall ask, it shall be done for them of my Father which is in heaven."*
>
> **Matthew 18:19**

It is only what is done now that counts. The present moment does not recede into the past. It advances into the future to confront us, spent or invested. Thought is the coin of heaven. Money is its earthly symbol. Every moment must be invested, and our inner talking reveals whether we are spending or investing. Be more interested in what you are inwardly "saying now" than what you "have said" by choosing wisely what you think and what you feel now.

Any time we feel misunderstood, misused, neglected, suspicious, afraid, we are spending our thoughts and wasting our time. Whenever we assume the feeling of being what we want to be, we are investing. We cannot abandon the moment to negative inner talking and expect to retain command of life. Before us go the results of all that seemingly is behind. Not gone is the last moment—but oncoming.

> *"My word shall not return unto me void, but it shall accomplish that which I please, and it shall prosper in the thing whereto I sent it."*
>
> **Isaiah 55:11**

The circumstances of life are the muffled utterances of the inner talking that made them—the word made visible.

> *"The Word", said Hermes, "is Son, and the Mind is Father of the Word. They are not separate one from the other; for life is the union of Word and Mind."*
>
> *"He willed us forth from Himself by the Word of Truth."*
>
> **James 1:18**

> *"Let us be imitators of God as dear children"*
>
> EPHESIANS 5:1

and use our inner speech wisely to mould an outer world in harmony with our ideal.

> *"The Lord spake by me, and his word was in my tongue."*
>
> 2 SAMUEL 23:2

The mouth of God is the mind of man. Feed God only the best.

> *"Whatsoever things are of good report... think on these things."*
>
> PHILIPPIANS 4:8

The present moment is always precisely right for an investment, to inwardly speak the right word.

> *"The word is very near to you, in your mouth, and in your heart, that you may do it. See, I have set before you this day life and good, death and evil, blessings and cursings. Choose life."*
>
> DEUTERONOMY 30:14, 15, 19

You choose life and good and blessings by being that which you choose. Like is known to like alone. Make your inner speech bless and give good reports. Man's ignorance of the future is the result of his ignorance of his inner talking. His inner talking mirrors his imagination, and his imagination is a government in which the opposition never comes into power.

If the reader asks, "What if the inner speech remains subjective and is unable to find an object for its love?" the answer is: it will not remain subjective, for the very simple reason that inner speech is always objectifying itself. What frustrates and festers and becomes the disease that afflicts humanity is man's ignorance of the art of matching inner words to fulfilled desire. Inner speech mirrors imagination, and imagination is Christ.

Alter your inner speech, and your perceptual world changes. Whenever inner speech and desire are in conflict, inner speech invariably wins.

Because inner speech objectifies itself, it is easy to see that if it matches desire, desire will be objectively realized. Were this not so, I would say with Blake

> *"Sooner murder an infant in its cradle than nurse unacted desires."*

But I know from experience

> *"The tongue... setteth on fire the course of nature."*
>
> JAMES 3:6

6

# It is Within

> *...Rivers, Mountains, Cities, Villages,*
> *All are Human, & when you enter into their Bosoms you walk In Heavens & Earths, as in your own Bosom you bear your Heaven And Earth & all you behold; tho' it appears Without, it is Within, In your Imagination, of which this World of Mortality is but a Shadow.*
>
> BLAKE, JERUSALEM

The inner world was as real to Blake as the outer land of waking life. He looked upon his dreams and visions as the realities of the forms of nature. Blake reduced everything to the bedrock of his own consciousness.

> *The Kingdom of Heaven is within you.*
>
> LUKE 17:21

The Real Man, the Imaginative Man, has invested the outer world with all of its properties. The apparent reality of the outer world which is so hard to dissolve is only proof of the absolute reality of the inner world of his own imagination.

*No man can come to me, except the Father which hath sent me draw him... I and my Father are one."*

**John 6:44; 10:30**

The world which is described from observation is a manifestation of the mental activity of the observer. When man discovers that his world is his own mental activity made visible, that no man can come unto him except he draws him, and that there is no one to change but himself, his own imaginative self, his first impulse is to reshape the world in the image of his ideal. But his ideal is not so easily incarnated. In that moment when he ceases to conform to external discipline, he must impose upon himself a far more rigorous discipline, the self-discipline upon which the realization of his ideal depends.

Imagination is not entirely untrammelled and free to move at will without any rules to constrain it. In fact, the contrary is true. Imagination travels according to habit. Imagination has choice, but it chooses according to habit. Awake or asleep, man's imagination is constrained to follow certain definite patterns. It is this benumbing influence of habit that man must change; if he does not, his dreams will fade under the paralysis of custom.

Imagination, which is Christ in man, is not subject to the necessity to produce only that which is perfect and good. It exercises its absolute freedom from necessity by endowing the outer physical self with free will to choose to follow good or evil, order or disorder.

*"Choose this day whom ye will serve."*

**Joshua 24:15**

But after the choice is made and accepted, so that it forms the individual's habitual consciousness, then imagination manifests its infinite power and wisdom by moulding the outer sensuous world of becoming in the image of the habitual inner speech and actions of the individual.

To realize his ideal, man must first change the pattern which his imagination has followed. Habitual thought is indicative of character. The way to change the outer world is to make the inner speech and action match the outer speech and action of fulfilled desire.

Our ideals are waiting to be incarnated, but unless we ourselves match our inner speech and action to the speech and action of fulfilled desire, they are incapable of birth. Inner speech and action are the channels of God's action. He cannot respond to our prayer unless these paths are offered. The outer behaviour of man is mechanical. It is subject to the compulsion applied to it by the behaviour of the inner self, and old habits of the inner self hang on till replaced by new ones. It is a peculiar property of the second or inner man that he gives to the outer self, something similar to his own reality of being. Any change in the behaviour of the inner self will result in corresponding outer changes.

The mystic calls a change of consciousness "death". By death he means, not the destruction of imagination and the state with which it was fused, but the dissolution of their union. Fusion is union rather than oneness. Thus the conditions to which that union gave being vanish. "I die daily", said Paul to the Corinthians. Blake said to his friend Crabbe Robinson:

> *There is nothing like death. Death is the best thing that can happen in life; but most people die so late and take such an unmerciful time in dying. God knows, their neighbors never see them rise from the dead.*

To the outer man of sense, who knows nothing of the inner man of Being, this is sheer nonsense. But Blake made the above quite clear when he wrote in the year before he died:

> *William Blake—one who is very much delighted with being in good company. Born 28 November 1757 in London and has died several times since.*

When man has the sense of Christ as his imagination, he sees why Christ must die and rise again from the dead to save man—why he must detach his imagination from his present state and match it to a higher concept of himself if he would rise above his present limitations and thereby save himself.

Here is a lovely story of a mystical death which was witnessed by a "neighbor". "Last week", writes the one "who rose from the dead", "a friend offered me her home in the mountains for the Christmas holidays as she thought she might go east. She said that she would let me know this week. We had a very pleasant conversation and I mentioned you and your teaching in connection with a discussion of Dunne's 'Experiment with Time' which she had been reading.

"Her letter arrived Monday. As I picked it up, I had a sudden sense of depression. However, when I read it, she said I could have the house and told me where to get the keys. Instead of being cheerful, I grew still more depressed, so much so I decided there must have been something between the lines which I was getting intuitively. I unfolded the letter and read the first page through and as I turned to the second page, I noticed she had written a postscript on the back of the first sheet. It consisted of an extremely blunt and heavy-handed description of an unlovely trait in my character which I had struggled for years to overcome, and for the past two years I thought I had succeeded. Yet here it was again, described with clinical exactitude.

"I was stunned and desolated. I thought to myself, 'What is this letter trying to tell me? In the first place, she invited me to use her house, as I have been seeing myself in some lovely home during the holidays. In the second place, nothing comes to me except I draw it. And thirdly I have been hearing nothing but good news. So the obvious conclusion is that something in me corresponds to this letter and no matter what it looks like it is good news.

"I reread the letter and as I did so, I asked, 'What is there here for me to see?' "And then I saw. It started out, 'After our conversation of last week, I feel I can tell you…' and the rest of the page was as studded with 'weres' and 'wases' as currants in a seed cake. "A great feeling of elation swept over me. It was all in the past. The thing I had laboured so long to correct was done. I suddenly realized that my friend was a witness to my resurrection.

I whirled around the studio, chanting, 'It's all in the past! It is done. Thank you, it is done!'I gathered all my gratitude up in a big ball of light and shot it straight to you and if you saw a flash of lightning Monday evening shortly after six your time, that was it.

"Now, instead of writing a polite letter because it is the correct thing to do, I can write giving sincere thanks for her frankness and thanking her for the loan of her house. Thank you so much for your teaching, which has made my beloved imagination truly my Saviour."

And now, if any man shall say unto her

> *"Lo, here is Christ, or there",*

she will believe it not, for she knows that the Kingdom of God is within her and that she herself must assume full responsibility for the incarnation of her ideal and that nothing but death and resurrection will bring her to it. She has found her Saviour, her beloved Imagination, forever expanding in the bosom of God.

There is only one reality, and that is Christ—Human Imagination, the inheritance and final achievement of the whole of Humanity,

> *That we... speaking the truth in love, may grow up into Him in all things, which is the head, even Christ."*

# 7

# Creation is Finished

*I am the beginning and the end, there is nothing to come that has not been, and is.*

ECCLESIASTES 3:15 ERV

Blake saw all possible human situations as "already-made" states. He saw every aspect, every plot and drama as already worked out as "mere possibilities" as long as we are not in them, but as overpowering realities when we are in them. He described these states as "Sculptures of Los's Halls".

*Distinguish therefore states from Individuals in those States.*
*States change but Individual Identities never change nor cease...*
*The Imagination is not a State.*

Said Blake,

*It is the Human Existence itself. Affection or Love becomes a State when divided from imagination.*

Just how important this is to remember is almost impossible to say, but the moment the individual realizes this for the first time is the most momentous in his life, and to be encouraged to feel this is the highest form of encouragement it is possible to give.

This truth is common to all men, but the consciousness of it, and much more, the self-consciousness of it, is another matter.

The day I realized this great truth, that everything in my world is a manifestation of the mental activity which goes on within me, and that the conditions and circumstances of my life only reflect the state of consciousness with which I am fused, is the most momentous in my life. But the experience that brought me to this certainty is so remote from ordinary existence, I have long hesitated to tell it, for my reason refused to admit the conclusions to which the experience impelled me. Nevertheless, this experience revealed to me that I am supreme within the circle of my own state of consciousness and that it is the state with which I am identified that determines what I experience. Therefore it should be shared with all, for to know this is to become free from the world's greatest tyranny, the belief in a second cause.

> *Blessed are the pure in heart: for they shall see God.*
>
> MATTHEW 5:8

Blessed are they whose imagination has been so purged of the beliefs in second causes they know that imagination is all, and all is imagination.

One day I quietly slipped from my apartment in New York City into some remote yesteryear's countryside. As I entered the dining room of a large inn, I became fully conscious. I knew that my physical body was immobilized on my bed back in New York. Yet here I was as awake and as conscious as I have ever been. I intuitively knew that if I could stop the activity of my mind, everything before me would freeze. No sooner was the thought born than the urge to try it possessed me. I felt my head tighten, then thicken to a stillness. My attention concentrated into a crystal-clear focus, and the waitress walking, walked not. And I looked through the window and the leaves falling, fell not. And the family of four eating, ate not. And they lifting the food, lifted it not. Then my attention relaxed, the tightness eased, and of a sudden all moved onward in their course. The leaves fell, the waitress walked and the family ate. Then I understood Blake's vision of the "Sculptures of Los's Halls".

*I sent you to reap that whereon ye bestowed no labor.*

**John 4:38**

Creation is finished.

*"I am the beginning and the end, there is nothing to come that has not been, and is."*

**Ecclesiastes 3:15, ERV**

The world of creation is finished and its original is within us. We saw it before we set forth, and have since been trying to remember it and to activate sections of it. There are infinite views of it. Our task is to get the right view and by determined direction of our attention make it pass in procession before the inner eye. If we assemble the right sequence and experience it in imagination until it has the tone of reality, then we consciously create circumstances. This inner procession is the activity of imagination that must be consciously directed. We, by a series of mental transformations, become aware of increasing portions of that which already is, and by matching our own mental activity to that portion of creation which we desire to experience, we activate it, resurrect it, and give it life.

This experience of mine not only shows the world as a manifestation of the mental activity of the individual observer, but it also reveals our course of time as jumps of attention between eternal moments. An infinite abyss separates any two moments of ours. We, by the movements of our attention, give life to the "Sculptures of Los's Halls".

Think of the world as containing an infinite number of states of consciousness from which it could be viewed. Think of these states as rooms or mansions in the House of God, and like the rooms of any house, they are fixed relative to one another. But think of yourself, the Real Self, the Imaginative You, as the living, moving occupant of God's House. Each room contains some of Los's Sculptures, with infinite plots and dramas and situations already worked out but not activated. They are activated as soon as Human Imagination enters and fuses with them. Each represents certain mental and emotional activities. To enter a state, man must consent to the ideas and feelings which it represents. These states represent an infinite number of possible mental transformations which man can experience. To move into another state or mansion necessitates a change of beliefs. All that you could ever desire is already present and only waits to be matched by your beliefs. But it must be matched, for that is the necessary condition by which alone it can be activated and objectified. Matching the beliefs of a state is the seeking that finds, the knocking to which it is opened, the asking that receives. Go in and possess the land.

The moment man matches the beliefs of any state, he fuses with it, and this union results in the activation and projection of its plots, plans, dramas, and situations. It becomes the individual's home from which he views the world. It is his workshop, and, if he is observant, he will see outer reality shaping itself upon the model of his... Imagination.

It is for this purpose of training us in image-making that we were made subject to the limitations of the senses and clothed in bodies of flesh. It is the awakening of the imagination, the returning of His Son, that our Father waits for.

> *"The creature was made subject to vanity not willingly, but by reason of him who subjected it."*
>
> **Romans 8:20**

But the victory of the Son, the return of the prodigal, assures us that

> *the creature shall be delivered from the bondage of corruption into the glorious liberty of the Sons of God."*
>
> **Romans 8:21**

We were subjected to this biological experience because no one can know of imagination who has not been subjected to the vanities and limitations of the flesh, who has not taken his share of Sonship and gone prodigal, who has not experimented and tasted this cup of experience; and confusion will continue until man awakes and a fundamentally imaginative view of life has been re-established and acknowledged as basic.

*"I should preach… the unsearchable riches of Christ and make all men see what is the fellowship of the mystery, which from the beginning of the world has been hid in God, Who created all things by Jesus Christ."*

EPHESIANS 3:8, 9

Bear in mind that Christ in you is your imagination.

As the appearance of our world is determined by the particular state with which we are fused, so may we determine our fate as individuals by fusing our imaginations with ideals we seek to realize. On the distinction between our states of consciousness depends the distinction between the circumstances and conditions of our lives. Man, who is free in his choice of state, often cries out to be saved from the state of his choice.

*"And ye shall cry out in that day, because of your king which ye shall have chosen you; and the Lord will not hear you in that day. Nevertheless, the people refused to obey the voice of Samuel; and they said, Nay; but we will have a king over us."*

EPHESIANS 3:8, 9

Choose wisely the state that you will serve. All states are lifeless until imagination fuses with them.

*"All things when they are admitted are made manifest by the light: for everything that is made manifest is light,"*

EPHESIANS 5:13

And

*"Ye are the light of the world,"*

MATTHEW 5:14

by which those ideas to which you have consented are made manifest.

Hold fast to your ideal. Nothing can take it from you but your imagination. Don't think of your ideal, think from it. It is only the ideals from which you think that are ever realized.

> *"Man lives not by bread alone, but by every word that proceeds out of the mouth of God"*
>
> MATTHEW 4:4

and "the mouth of God" is the mind of man.

Become a drinker and an eater of the ideals you wish to realize. Have a set, definite aim or your mind will wander, and wandering it eats every negative suggestion. If you live right mentally, everything else will be right. By a change of mental diet, you can alter the course of observed events. But unless there is a change of mental diet, your personal history remains the same. You illuminate or darken your life by the ideas to which you consent. Nothing is more important to you than the ideas on which you feed. And you feed on the ideas from which you think. If you find the world unchanged, it is a sure sign that you are wanting in fidelity to the new mental diet, which you neglect in order to condemn your environment. You are in need of a new and sustained attitude. You can be anything you please if you will make the conception habitual, for any idea which excludes all others from the field of attention discharges in action. The ideas and moods to which you constantly return define the state with which you are fused. Therefore train yourself to occupy more frequently the feeling of your wish fulfilled. This is creative magic. It is the way to work toward fusion with the desired state.

If you would assume the feeling of your wish fulfilled more frequently, you would be master of your fate, but unfortunately you shut out your assumption for all but the occasional hour. Practice making real to yourself the feeling of the wish fulfilled. After you have assumed the feeling of the wish fulfilled, do not close the experience as you would a book, but carry it around like a fragrant odor. Instead of being completely forgotten, let it remain in the atmosphere communicating its influence automatically to your actions and reactions. A mood, often repeated, gains a momentum that is hard to break or check. So be careful of the feelings you entertain. Habitual moods reveal the state with which you are fused.

It is always possible to pass from thinking of the end you desire to realize, to thinking from the end. But the crucial matter is thinking from the end, for thinking from means unification or fusion with the idea: whereas in thinking of the end, there is always subject and object—the thinking individual and the thing thought. You must imagine yourself into the state of your wish fulfilled, in your love for that state, and in so doing, live and think from it and no more of it. You pass from thinking of to thinking from by centering your imagination in the feeling of the wish fulfilled.

8

# *The Apple of God's Eye*

*"What think ye of the Christ? Whose Son is He?"*

**Matthew 22:42**

When this question is asked of you, let your answer be, "Christ is my imagination," and, though I

*See not yet all things put under him,*

**Hebrews 2:8**

yet I know that I am Mary from whom sooner or later He shall be born, and eventually

*"Do all things through Christ."*

The birth of Christ is the awakening of the inner or Second man. It is becoming conscious of the mental activity within oneself, which activity continues whether we are conscious of it or not.

The birth of Christ does not bring any person from a distance, or make anything to be that was not there before. It is the unveiling of the Son of God in man. The Lord "cometh in clouds" is the prophet's description of the pulsating rings of golden liquid light on the head of him in whom He awakes. The coming is from within and not from without, as Christ is in us.

This great mystery

*God was manifest in the flesh*

begins with Advent, and it is appropriate that the cleansing of the Temple,

*"Which temple ye are,"*

1 CORINTHIANS 3:17

stands in the forefront of the Christian mysteries.

*"The Kingdom of Heaven is within you."*

LUKE 17:21

Advent is unveiling the mystery of your being. If you will practice the art of revision by a life lived according to the wise, imaginative use of your inner speech and inner actions, in confidence that by the conscious use of "the power that worketh in us," Christ will awake in you; if you believe it, trust it, act upon it; Christ will awake in you. This is Advent.

*"Great is the mystery, God was manifest in the flesh."*

1 TIMOTHY 3:16

From Advent on,

*"He that toucheth you toucheth the apple of God's eye."*

ZECHARIAH 2:8

2

# Be What You Wish

# *Introduction*

Most men are totally unaware of the creative power of imagination and invariably bow before the dictates of 'facts' and accepts life on the basis of the world without. But when you discover this creative power within yourself, you will boldly assert the supremacy of imagination and put all things in subjection to it.

It is believed that all men can change the course of their lives. By our imagination, by our affirmations, we can change our world, we can change our future. If we strive passionately to embody a new and higher concept of ourselves, then all things will be at our service.

# 1

# *Be What You Wish*

A newspaperman related to me that our great scientist, Robert Millikan, once told him that he had set a goal for himself at an early age when he was still very poor and unproven in the great work he was to do in the future. He condensed his dream of greatness and security into a simple statement, which statement, implied that his dream of greatness and security was already realized. Then he repeated the statement over and over again to himself until the idea of greatness and security filled his mind and crowded all other ideas out of his consciousness. These may not have been the words of Dr. Millikan but they are those given to me and I quote, "I have a lavish, steady, dependable income, consistent with integrity and mutual benefit." As I have said repeatedly, everything depends upon our attitude towards ourselves. That which we will not affirm as true of ourselves cannot develop in our life. Dr. Millikan wrote his dream of greatness and security in the first person, present tense. He did not say, "I will be great; I will be secure," for that would have implied that he was not great and secure. Instead, he made his future dream a present fact. "I have," said he, "a lavish, steady, dependable income, consistent with integrity and mutual benefit."

The future dream must become a present fact in the mind of him who seeks to realize it. We must experience in imagination what we would experience in reality in the event we achieved our goal, for the soul imagining itself into a situation takes on the results of that imaginary act. If it does not imagine itself into a situation, it is ever free of the result.

It is the purpose of this teaching to lift us to a higher state of consciousness, to stir the highest in us to confidence and self-assertion, for that which stirs the highest in us is our teacher and healer. The very first word of correction or cure is always, "Arise." If we are to understand the reason for this constant command of the Bible to "arise," we must recognize that the universe understood internally is an infinite series of levels and man is what he is according to where he is in that series. As we are lifted up in consciousness, our world reshapes itself in harmony with the level to which we are lifted. He who raises from his prayer a better man, his prayer has been granted.

To change the present state we, like Dr. Millikan, must rise to a higher level of consciousness. This rise is accomplished by affirming that we are already that which we want to be; by assuming the feeling of the wish fulfilled. The drama of life is a psychological one which we bring to pass by our attitudes rather than by our acts. There is no escape from our present predicament except by a radical psychological transformation. Everything depends upon our attitude towards ourselves. That which we will not affirm as true of ourselves will not develop in our lives.

We hear much of the humble man, the meek man – but what is meant by a meek man? He is not poor and groveling, the proverbial doormat, as he is generally conceived to be. Men who make themselves as worms in their own sight have lost the vision of that life – into the likeness of which it is the true purpose of the spirit to transform this life. Men should take their measurements not from life as they see it but from men like Dr. Millkan, who, while poor and unproven, dared to assume, "I have a lavish, steady, dependable income, consistent with integrity and mutual benefit." Such men are the meek of the Gospels, the men who inherit the earth. Any concept of self less than the best robs us of the earth. The promise is, "Blessed are the meek, for they shall inherit the earth." In the original text, the word translated as meek is the opposite of the words –

resentful – angry. It has the meaning of becoming "tamed" as a wild animal is tamed. After the mind is tamed, it may be likened to a vine, of which it may be said, "Behold this vine. I found it a wild tree whose wanton strength had swollen into irregular twigs. But I pruned the plant, and it grew temperate in its vain expense of useless leaves, and knotted as you see into these clean, full clusters to repay the hand that wisely wounded it."

A meek man is a self-disciplined man. He is so disciplined he sees only the finest, he thinks only the best. He is the one who fulfills the suggestion, "Brethren, whatsoever things are true, whatsoever things are honest, whatsoever things are just, whatsoever things are pure, whatsoever things are lovely, whatsoever things are of good report; if there be any virtue and if there be any praise, think on these things."

We rise to a higher level of consciousness, not because we have curbed our passions, but because we have cultivated our virtues. In truth, a meek man is a man in complete control of his moods, and his moods are the highest, for he knows he must keep a high mood if he would walk with the highest.

It is my belief that all men can, like Dr. Millikan, change the course of their lives. I believe that Dr. Millikan's technique of making his desire a present fact to himself is of great importance to any seeker after the "truth." It is also his high purpose to be of "mutual benefit" that is inevitably the goal of us all. It is much easier to imagine the good of all than to be purely selfish in our imagining. By our imagination, by our affirmations, we can change our world, we can change our future. To the man of high purpose, to the disciplined man, this is a natural measure, so let us all become disciplined men. Next Sunday morning, July 15th, I am speaking as the guest of Dr. Bailes at 10:30 at the Fox-Wilshire Theater on Wilshire Boulevard, near La Cienega. My subject for next Sunday is "Changing Your Future." It is a subject near to the hearts of us all. I hope you will all come on Sunday to learn how to be the disciplined man, the meek man, who "changes his future" to the benefit of his fellow man. If you are observant, you will notice the swift echo or response to your every mood in this message and you will be able to key it to the circumstances of your daily life.

When we are certain of the relationship of mood to circumstance in our lives, we welcome what befalls us. We know that all we meet is part of ourselves. In the creation of a new life we must begin at the beginning, with a change of mood. Every high mood of man is the opening of the door to a higher level for him. Let us mould our lives about a high mood or a community of high moods. Individuals, as well as communities, grow spiritually in proportion as they rise to a higher ideal. If their ideal is lowered, they sink to its depths; if their ideal is exalted, they are elevated to heights unimagined. We must keep the high mood if we would walk with the highest; the heights, also, were meant for habitation. All forms of the creative imagination imply elements of feeling. Feeling is the ferment without which no creation is possible. There is nothing wrong with our desire to transcend our present state. There would be no progress in this world were it not for man's dissatisfaction with himself. It is natural for us to seek a more beautiful personal life; it is right that we wish for greater understanding, greater health, greater security. It is stated in the sixteenth chapter of the Gospel of St. John, "Heretofore have ye asked for nothing in my name; ask and ye shall receive, that your joy may be full."

A spiritual revival is needed for mankind, but by spiritual revival I mean a true religious attitude, one in which each individual, himself, accepts the challenge of embodying a new and higher value of himself as Dr. Millikan did. A nation can exhibit no greater wisdom in the mass than it generates in its units. For this reason, I have always preached self-help, knowing that if we strive passionately after this kind of self-help, that is, to embody a new and higher concept of ourselves, then all other kinds of help will be at our service.

The ideal we serve and hope to achieve is ready for a new incarnation; but unless we offer it human parentage it is incapable of birth. We must affirm that we are already that which we hope to be and live as though we were, knowing like Dr. Millikan, that our assumption, though false to the outer world, if persisted in, will harden into fact.

The perfect man judges not after appearances; he judges righteously. He sees himself and others as he desires himself and them to be. He hears what he wants to hear. He sees and hears only the good. He knows the truth, and the truth sets him free and leads him to good. The truth shall set all mankind free. This is our spiritual revival. Character is largely the result of the direction and persistence of voluntary attention.

*"Think truly, and thy thoughts shall the world's famine feed;*
*Speak truly, and each word of thine shall be a fruitful seed;*
*Live truly, and thy life shall be a great and noble creed."*

2

# *By Imagination We Become*

How many times have we heard someone say, "Oh, it's only his imagination?" *Only his imagination* – man's imagination is the man himself. No man has too little imagination, but few men have disciplined their imagination. Imagination is itself indestructible. Therein lies the horror of its misuse. Daily, we pass some stranger on the street and observe him muttering to himself, carrying on an imaginary argument with one not present. He is arguing with vehemence, with fear or with hatred, not realizing that he is setting in motion, *by his imagination*, an unpleasant event which he will presently encounter.

The world, as imagination sees it, is the real world. Not facts, but figments of the imagination, shape our daily lives. It is the exact and literal minded who live in a fictitious world. Only imagination can restore the Eden from which experience has driven us out. Imagination is the sense by which we perceived the above, the power by which we resolve vision into being. Every stage of man's progress is made by the exercise of the imagination. It is only because men do not perfectly imagine and believe that their results are sometimes uncertain when they might always be perfectly certain. Determined imagination is the beginning of all successful operation. The imagination, alone, is the means of fulfilling the intention. The man who, at will, can call up whatever image he pleases is, by virtue of the power of his imagination, least of all subject to caprice. The solitary or captive can, by intensity of imagination and feeling, affect myriads so that he can act through many men and speak through many voices. "We should never be certain," wrote William Butler Yeats in his *Ideas of Good and Evil*, "that it was not some woman treading in the wine-press who began that subtle change in men's minds, or that the passion did not begin in the mind of some shepherd boy, lighting up his eyes for a moment before it ran upon its way."

Let me tell you the story of a very dear friend of mine, at the time the costume designer of the Music Hall in New York. She told me, one day, of her difficulty in working with one of the producers who invariably criticized and rejected her best work unjustly; that he was often rude and seemed deliberately unfair to her. Upon hearing her story, I reminded her, as I am reminding you, that men can only echo to us that which we whisper to them in secret. I had no doubt but that she silently argued with the producer, not in the flesh, but in quiet moments to herself. She confessed that she did just that each morning as she walked to work. I asked her to change her attitude toward him, to assume that he was congratulating her on her fine designs and she, in turn, was thanking him for his praise and kindness. This young designer took my advice and as she walked to the theater, she imagined a perfect relationship of the producer praising her work and she, in turn, responding with gratitude for his appreciation. This she did morning after morning and in a very short while, she discovered for herself that her own attitude determined the scenery of her existence. The behavior of the producer completely reversed itself. He became the most pleasant professional employer she had encountered. His behavior merely echoed the changes that she had whispered within herself. What she did was by the power of imagination. Her fantasy led his; and she, herself, dictated to him the discourse they eventually had together at the time she was seemingly walking alone.

Let us set ourselves, here and now, a daily exercise of controlling and disciplining our imagination. What finer beginning than to imagine better than the best we know for a friend. There is no coal of character so dead that it will not glow and flame if but slightly turned. Don't blame; only resolve. Life, like music, can by a new setting turn all its discords into harmonies. Represent your friend to yourself as already expressing that which he desires to be. Let us know that with whatever attitude we approach another, a similar attitude approaches us.

How can we do this? Do what my friend did. To establish rapport, call your friend mentally. Focus your attention on him and mentally call his name just as you would to attract his attention were you to see him on the street. Imagine that he has answered, mentally hear his voice – imagine that he is telling you of the great good you have desired for him. You, in turn, tell him of your joy in witnessing his good fortune. Having mentally heard that which you wanted to hear, having thrilled to the news heard, go about your daily task. Your imagined conversation must awaken what it affirmed; the acceptance of the end wills the means. And the wisest reflection could not devise more effective means than those which are willed by the acceptance of the end.

However, your conversation with your friend must be in a manner which does not express the slightest doubt as to the truth of what you imagine that you hear and say. If you do not control your imagination, you will find that you are hearing and saying all that you formerly heard and said. We are creatures of habit; and habit, though not law, acts like the most compelling law in the world. With this knowledge of the power of imagination, be as the disciplined man and transform your world by imagining and feeling only what is lovely and of good report. The beautiful idea you awaken in yourself shall not fail to arouse its affinity in others. Do not wait four months for the harvest. Today is the day to practice the control and discipline of your imagination. Man is only limited by weakness of attention and poverty of imagination. The great secret is a controlled imagination and a well sustained attention, firmly and repeatedly focused on the object to be accomplished.

"Now is the acceptable time to give beauty for ashes, joy for mourning, praise for the spirit of heaviness; that they might be called trees of righteousness, the planting of the Lord that He might be glorified."

Now is the time to control our imagination and attention. By control, I do not mean restraint by will power but rather cultivation through love and compassion. With so much of the world in discord we cannot possibly emphasize too strongly the power of imaginative love. Imaginative Love, that is my subject next Sunday morning when I shall speak for Dr. Bailes while he is on his holiday. The services will be held as always at the Fox Wilshire Theater on Wilshire Boulevard, near La Cienega at 10:30. "As the world is, so is the individual," should be changed to, "As the individual is so is the world." And I hope to be able to bring to each of you present the true meaning of the words of Zechariah, "Speak ye every man the truth to his neighbor and let none of you imagine evil in your hearts against his neighbor." What a wonderful challenge to you and to me. "As a man thinketh in his heart so is he." As a man imagines so is he. Hold fast to love in your imagination. By creating an ideal within your mental sphere you can approximate yourself to this "ideal image" till you become one and the same with it, thereby transforming yourself into it, or rather, absorbing its qualities into the very core of your being. Never, never, lose sight of the power that is within you. Imaginative love lifts the invisible into sight and gives us water in the desert. It builds for the soul its only fit abiding place. Beauty, love and all of good report are the garden, but imaginative love is the way into the garden.

*Sow an imaginary conversation, you reap an act;*
*Sow an act, you reap a habit;*
*Sow a habit, you reap a character;*
*Sow a character, you reap your destiny.*

By imagination, we are all reaping our destinies, whether they be good, bad, or indifferent. Imagination has full power of objective realization and every stage of man's progress or regression is made by the exercise of imagination. I believe with William Blake, "What seems to be, is, to those to whom it seems to be, and is productive of the most dreadful consequences to those to whom it seems to be, even of torments, despair, and eternal death. By imagination and desire we become what we desire to be. Let us affirm to ourselves that we are what we imagine. If we persist in the assumption that we are what we wish to be, we will become transformed into that which we have imagined ourselves to be. We were born by a natural miracle of love and for a brief space of time our needs were all another's care. In that simple truth lies the secret of life. Except by love, we cannot truly live at all. Our parents in their separate individualities have no power to transmit life. So, back we come to the basic truth that life is the offspring of love. Therefore, no love, no life. Thus, it is rational to say that, "God is Love."

Love is our birthright. Love is the fundamental necessity of our life. "Do not go seeking for that which you are. Those who go seeking for love only make manifest their own lovelessness and the loveless never find love. Only the loving find love and they never have to seek for it."

## 3

# *Answered Prayer*

Have you ever had a prayer answered? What wouldn't men give just to feel certain that when they pray, something definite would happen. For this reason, I would like to take a little time to see why it is that some prayers are answered and some apparently fall on dry ground. "When ye pray, believe that ye receive, and ye shall receive." Believe that ye receive – is the condition imposed upon man. Unless we believe that we receive, our prayer will not be answered. A prayer – granted – implies that something is done in consequence of the prayer which otherwise would not have been done. Therefore, the one who prays is the spring of action – the directing mind – and the one who grants the prayer. Such responsibility man refuses to assume, for responsibility it seems, is mankind's invisible nightmare.

The whole natural world is built on law. Yet, between prayer and its answer we see no such relation. We feel that God may answer or ignore our prayer, that our prayer may hit the mark or may miss it. The mind is still unwilling to admit that God subjects Himself to His own laws. How many people believe that there is, between prayer and its answer, a relation of cause and effect?

Let us take a look at the means employed to heal the ten lepers as related in the seventeenth chapter of the Gospel of St. Luke. The thing that strikes us in this story is the method that was used to raise their faith to the needful intensity. We are told that the ten lepers appealed to Jesus to "have mercy" on them – that is – to heal them. Jesus ordered them to go and show themselves to the priests, and "as they went, they were cleansed." The Mosaic Law demanded that when a leper recovered from his disease he must show himself to the priest to obtain a certificate of restored health. Jesus imposed a test upon the lepers' faith and supplied a means by which their faith could be raised to its full potency. If the lepers refused to go – they had no faith – and, therefore, could not be healed. But, if they obeyed Him, the full realization of what their journey implied would break upon their minds as they went and this dynamic thought would heal them. So, we read, "As they went, they were cleansed."

You, no doubt, often have heard the words of that inspiring old hymn – "Oh, what peace we often forfeit; oh, what needless pain we bear, all because we do not carry everything to God in prayer." I, myself, came to this conviction through experience, being led to brood upon the nature of prayer. I believe in the practice and philosophy of what men call prayer, but not everything that receives that name is really prayer.

Prayer is the elevation of the mind to that which we seek. The very first word of correction is always "arise." Always lift the mind to that which we seek. This is easily done by assuming the feeling of the wish fulfilled. How would you feel if your prayer were answered? Well, assume that feeling until you experience in imagination what you would experience in reality if your prayer were answered. Prayer means getting into action mentally. It means holding the attention upon the idea of the wish fulfilled until it fills the mind and crowds all other ideas out of the consciousness. This statement that prayer means getting into action mentally and holding the attention upon the idea of the wish fulfilled until it fills the mind and crowds all other ideas out of the consciousness, does not mean that prayer is a mental effort – an act of will. On the contrary, prayer is to be contrasted with an act of will. Prayer is a surrender. It means abandoning oneself to the feeling of the wish fulfilled. If prayer brings no response – there is something wrong with the prayer and the fault lies generally in too much effort. Serious confusion arises insofar as men identify the state of prayer with an act of will, instead of contrasting it with an act of will. The sovereign rule is to make no effort, and if this is observed, you will intuitively fall into the right attitude.

Creativeness is not an act of will, but a deeper receptiveness – a keener susceptibility. The acceptance of the end – the acceptance of the answered prayer – finds the means for its realization. Feel yourself into the state of the answered prayer until the state fills the mind and crowds all other states out of your consciousness. What we must work for is not the development of the will, but the education of the imagination and the steadying of attention. Prayer succeeds by avoiding conflict. Prayer is, above all things, easy. Its greatest enemy is effort. The mighty surrenders itself fully only to that which is most gentle. The wealth of Heaven may not be seized by a strong will, but surrenders itself, a free gift, to the God-spent moment. Along the lines of least resistance travel spiritual as well as physical forces.

We must act on the assumption that we already possess that which we desire, for all that we desire is already present within us. It only waits to be claimed. That it must be claimed is a necessary condition by which we realize our desires. Our prayers are answered if we assume the feeling of the wish fulfilled and continue in that assumption. One of the loveliest examples of an answered prayer I witnessed in my own living room. A very charming lady from out of town came to see me concerning prayer. As she had no one with whom to leave her eight-year old son, she brought him with her the time of our interview. Seemingly, he was engrossed in playing with a toy truck, but at the end of the interview with his mother he said, "Mr. Neville, I know how to pray now. I know what I want – a collie puppy – and I can imagine I am hugging him every night on my bed." His mother explained to him and to me the impossibilities of his prayer, the cost of the puppy, their confined home, even his inability to care for the dog properly. The boy looked into his mother's eyes and simply said, "But, Mother, I know how to pray now." And he did. Two months later during a "Kindness to Animals Week" in his city, all the school children were required to write an essay on how they would love and care for a pet.

You have guessed the answer. His essay, out of the five thousand submitted, won the prize, and that prize, presented by the mayor of the city to the lad – was a collie puppy. The boy truly assumed the feeling of his wish fulfilled, hugging and loving his puppy every night.

Prayer is an act of Imaginative Love which is to be the subject of my message next Sunday morning at 10:30 at the Fox Wilshire Theater on Wilshire Boulevard near La Cienega. It is my desire, next Sunday, that I may explain to you, how you, like the young boy; can yield yourselves to the lovely images of your desires and persist in your prayer even though you, like the lad, are told that your desires are impossible.

The necessity of persistence in prayer is shown us in the Bible. "Which of you," asked Jesus, "shall go unto him at midnight, and say unto him: Friend, lend me three loaves; for a friend of mine is come to me from a journey, and I have nothing to set before him; and he from within shall answer and say, 'Trouble me not; the door is now shut and my children are with me in bed; I cannot rise and give thee.' I say unto you, though he will not rise and give him because he is his friend, yet because of his importunity he will arise and give as many as he needeth." Luke 2. The word translated as "importunity" means, literally, shameless impudence. We must persist until we succeed in imagining ourselves into the situation of the answered prayer. The secret of success is found in the word "perseverance." The soul imagining itself into the act, takes on the results of the act. Not imagining itself into the act, it is ever free from the result. Experience in imagination what you would experience in reality were you already what you want to be, and you will take on the result of that act. Do not experience in imagination what you want to experience in reality and you will ever be free of the result. "When ye pray, believe that ye receive, and ye shall receive." One must persist until he reaches his friend on a higher level of consciousness. He must persist until his feeling of the wish fulfilled has all the sensory vividness of reality.

Prayer is a controlled waking dream. If we are to pray successfully, we must steady our attention to observe the world as it would be seen by us were our prayer answered.

Steadying attention makes no call upon any special faculty, but it does demand control of imagination. We must extend our senses – observe our changed relationship to our world and trust this observation. The new world is not there to grasp, but to sense, to touch. The best way to observe it is to be intensely aware of it. In other words, we can, by listening as though we heard and by looking as though we saw, actually hear voices and see scenes from within ourselves that are otherwise not audible or visible. With our attention focused on the state desired, the outer world crumbles and then the world – like music – by a new setting, turns all its discords into harmonies. Life is not a struggle but a surrender. Our prayers are answered by the powers we invoke not by those we exert. So long as the eyes take notice, the soul is blind – for the world that moves us is the one we imagine, not the world round about us. We must yield our whole being to the feeling of being the noble one we want to be. If anything is kept back, the prayer is vain. We often are deprived of our high goal by our effort to possess it. We are called upon to act on the assumption that we already are the man we would be. If we do this without effort – experiencing in imagination what we would experience in the flesh had we realized our goal, we shall find that we do, indeed, possess it. The healing touch is in our attitude. We need change nothing but our attitude towards it. Assume a virtue if you have it not, assume the feeling of your wish fulfilled. "Pray for my soul; more things are wrought by prayer than this world dreams of."

4

# Meditation

Many people tell me they cannot meditate. This seems to me a bit like saying they cannot play the piano after one attempt. Meditation, as in every art or expression, requires constant practice for perfect results. A truly great pianist, for instance, would feel he could not play his best if he missed one day of practice. If he missed a week or a month of practice he would know that even his most uninitiated audience would recognize his defects. So it is with meditation. If we practice daily with joy in this daily habit, we perfect it as an art. I find that those who complain of the difficulty in meditation do not make it a daily practice, but rather, wait until something pressing appears in their world and then, through an act of will, try to fix their attention on the desired state. But they do not know that meditation is the education of the will, for when will and imagination are in conflict, imagination invariably wins.

The dictionaries define meditation as fixing one's attention upon; as planning in the mind; as devising and looking forward; engaging in continuous and contemplative thought. A lot of nonsense has been written about meditation. Most books on the subject get the reader nowhere, for they do not explain the process of meditation. All that meditation amounts to is a controlled imagination and a well sustained attention. Simply hold the attention on a certain idea until it fills the mind and crowds all other ideas out of consciousness. The power of attention shows itself the sure guarantee of an inner force. We must concentrate on the idea to be realized, without permitting any distraction. This is the great secret of action. Should the attention wander, bring it back to the idea you wish to realize and do so again and again, until the attention becomes immobilized and undergoes an effortless fixation upon the idea presented to it. The idea must hold the attention – must fascinate it – so to speak. All meditation ends at last with the thinker, and he finds he is what he, himself, has conceived. The undisciplined man's attention is the servant of his vision rather than its master. It is captured by the pressing rather than the important.

In the act of meditation, as in the act of adoration, silence is our highest praise. Let us keep our silent sanctuaries, for in them the eternal perspectives are preserved. Day by day, week by week, year by year, at times where none through love or lesser intentions were allowed to interfere, I set myself to attain mastery over my attention and imagination. I sought out ways to make more securely my own, those magical lights that dawned and faded within me. I wished to evoke them at will and to be the master of my vision.

I would strive to hold my attention on the activities of the day in unwavering concentration so that, not for one moment, would the concentration slacken. This is an exercise – a training for higher adventures of the soul. It is no light labor. The ploughman's labor, working in the fields is easier by far.

Empires do not send legions so swiftly to obstruct revolt as all that is alive in us hurries along the nerve highways of the body to frustrate our meditative mood. The beautiful face of one we love glows before us to enchant us from our task. Old enmities and fears beleaguer us. If we are tempted down these vistas, we find, after an hour of musing, that we have been lured away. We have deserted our task and forgotten that fixity of attention we set out to achieve. What man is there who has complete control of his imagination and attention. A controlled imagination and steadied attention, firmly and repeatedly focused on the idea to be realized, is the beginning of all magical operations. If he persists through weeks and months, sooner or later, through meditation, he creates in himself a center of power. He will enter a path all may travel but on which few do journey. It is a path within himself where the feet first falter in shadow and darkness, but which later is made brilliant by an inner light. There is no need for special gifts or genius. It is not bestowed on any individual but won by persistence and practice of meditation. If he persists, the dark caverns of his brain will grow luminous and he will set out day after day for the hour of meditation as if to keep an appointment with a lover. When it comes, he rises within himself as a diver, too long under water, rises to breathe the air and see the light. In this meditative mood he experiences in imagination what he would experience in reality had he realized his goal, that he may in time become transformed into the image of his imagined state.

The only test of religion worth making is whether it is trueborn; whether it springs from the deepest consciousness of the individual; whether it is the fruit of experience; or whether it is anything else whatever. This is my reason for speaking to you on my last Sunday in Los Angeles about The True Religious Attitude. What is your religious attitude? What is my religious attitude? I shall speak on this subject next Sunday morning at 10:30 as Dr. Bailes' guest. The service will be held at the Fox Wilshire Theater on Wilshire Boulevard near La Cienega. I shall endeavor to show you that the methods of mental and spiritual knowledge are entirely different. For we know a thing mentally by looking at it from the outside, by comparing it with other things, by analyzing and defining it; whereas we can know a thing spiritually only by becoming it. We must be the thing itself and not merely talk about it or look at it. We must be in love if we are to know what love is. We must be God-like if we are to know what God is.

Meditation, like sleep, is an entrance into the subconscious. "When you pray, enter into your closet, and when you have shut your door, pray to your Father which is in secret and your Father which is in secret shall reward you openly." Meditation is an illusion of sleep which diminishes the impression of the outer world and renders the mind more receptive to suggestion from within. The mind in meditation is in a state of relaxation akin to the feeling attained just before dropping off to sleep. This state is beautifully described by the poet, Keats, in his ODE TO A NIGHTINGALE. It is said that as the poet sat in the garden and listened to the nightingale, he fell into a state which he described as "A drowsy numbness pains my senses as though of hemlock I had drunk." Then after singing his ode to the nightingale, Keats asked himself this question, "Was it a vision or a waking dream? Fled is the music; do I wake or sleep?" Those are the words of one who has seen something with such vividness or reality that he wonders whether the evidence of his physical eyes can now be believed.

Any kind of meditation in which we withdraw into ourselves without making too much effort to think is an outcropping of the subconscious. Think of the subconscious as a tide which ebbs and flows. In sleep, it is a flood tide, while at moments of full wakefulness, the tide is at its lowest ebb. Between these two extremes are any number of intermediary levels. When we are drowsy, dreamy, lulled in gentle reverie, the tide is high. The more wakeful and alert we become, the lower the tide sinks. The highest tide compatible with the conscious direction of our thoughts occurs just before we fall asleep and just after we wake. An easy way to create this passive state is to relax in a comfortable chair or on a bed. Close your eyes and imagine that you are sleepy, so sleepy, and so very sleepy. Act precisely as though you were going to take a siesta. In so doing, you allow the subconscious tide to rise to sufficient height to make your particular assumption effective.

When you first attempt this, you may find that all sorts of counter-thoughts try to distract you, but if you persist, you will achieve a passive state. When this passive state is reached, think only on "things of good report" – imagine that you are now expressing your highest ideal, not how you will express it, but simply feel *Here And Now* that you are the noble one you desire to be. You are it now. Call your high ideal into being by imagining and feeling you are it now.

I think all happiness depends on the energy to assume the feeling of the wish fulfilled, to assume the mask of some other more perfect life. If we cannot imagine ourselves different from what we are and try to assume that second more desirable self, we cannot impose a discipline upon ourselves though we may accept discipline from others.

Meditation is an activity of the soul; it is an active virtue; and an active virtue, as distinguished from passive acceptance of a code is theatrical. It is dramatic; it is the wearing of a mask. As your goal is accepted, you become totally indifferent to possible failure, for acceptance of the end wills the means to the end. When you emerge from the moment of meditation it is as though you were shown the happy end of a play in which you are the principal actor. Having witnessed the end in your meditation, regardless of any anti-climatic state you encounter, you remain calm and secure in the knowledge that the end has been perfectly defined.

Creation is finished and what we call creativeness is really only a deeper receptiveness or keener susceptibility on our part, and this receptiveness is "Not by might, nor by power, but by my spirit, saith the Lord of Hosts." Through meditation, we awaken within ourselves a center of light, which will be to us a pillar of cloud by day and a pillar of fire by night.

# 5

# *The Law of Assumption*

The great mystic, William Blake, wrote almost two hundred years ago, "What seems to be, is, to those to whom it seems to be and is productive of the most dreadful consequences to those to whom it seems to be." Now, at first, this mystical gem seems a bit involved, or at best to be a play on words; but it is nothing of the kind. Listen to it carefully. "What seems to be, is, to those to whom it seems to be." That is certainly clear enough. It is a simple truth about the law of assumption, and a warning of the consequences of its misuse. The author of the Epistle to the Romans declared in the fourteenth chapter, "I know, and am persuaded by the Lord Jesus, that there is nothing unclean of itself; but to him that esteemeth anything to be unclean, to him it is unclear."

We see by this that it is not superior insight but purblindness that reads into the greatness of men some littleness with which it chances to be familiar, for what seems to be, is, to those to whom it seems to be.

Experiments recently conducted at two of our leading universities revealed this great truth about the law of assumption. They stated in their releases to the newspapers, that after two thousand experiments they came to the conclusion that, 'What you see when you look at something depends not so much on what is there as on the assumption you make when you look. What you believe to be the real physical world is actually only an assumptive world." In other words, you would not define your husband in the same way that you mother would. Yet, you are both defining the same person. Your particular relationship to a thing influences your feelings with respect to that thing and makes you see in it an element which is not there. If your feeling in the matter is a self-element; it can be cast out. If it is a permanent distinction in the state considered, it cannot be cast out. The thing to do is to try. If you can change your opinion of another, then what you now believe of him cannot be absolutely true, but relatively true.

Men believe in the reality of the external world because they do not know how to focus and condense their powers to penetrate its thin crust. Strangely enough, it is not difficult to penetrate this view of the senses. To remove the veil of the senses, we do not employ great effort; the objective world vanishes as we turn our attention from it. We have only to concentrate on the state desired to mentally see it; but to give reality to it so that it will become an objective fact, we must focus our attention upon the desired state until it has all the sensory vividness and feeling of reality. When, through concentrated attention, our desire appears to possess the distinctness and feeling of reality; when the form of thought is as vivid as the form of nature, we have given it the right to become a visible fact in our lives. Each man must find the means best suited to his nature to control his attention and concentrate it on the desired state. I find for myself the best state to be one of meditation, a relaxed state akin to sleep, but a state in which I am still consciously in control of my imagination and capable of fixing my attention on a mental object.

If it is difficult to control the direction of your attention while in this state akin to sleep, you may find gazing fixedly into an object very helpful. Do not look at its surface, but rather into and beyond any plain object such as a wall, a carpet or any object which possesses depth. Arrange it to return as little reflection as possible. Imagine, then, that in this depth you are seeing and hearing what you want to see and hear until your attention is exclusively occupied by the imagined state.

At the end of your meditation, when you awake from your controlled waking dream you feel as though you had returned from a great distance. The visible world which you had shut out returns to consciousness and, by its very presence, informs you that you have been self-deceived into believing that the object of your contemplation was real; but if you remain faithful to your vision this sustained mental attitude will give reality to your visions and they will become visible concrete facts in your world.

Define your highest ideal and concentrate your attention upon this ideal until you identify yourself with it. Assume the feeling of being it – the feeling that would be yours were you now embodying it in your world. This assumption, though now denied by your senses, "if persisted in" – will become a fact in your world. You will know when you have succeeded in fixing the desired state in consciousness simply by looking mentally at the people you know. This is a wonderful check on yourself as your mental conversations are more revealing than your physical conversations are. If, in your mental conversations with others, you talk with them as you formerly did, then you have not changed your concept of self, for all changes of concepts of self result in a changed relationship to the world. Remember what was said earlier, "What you see when you look at something depends not so much on what is there as on the assumption you make when you look." Therefore, the assumption of the wish fulfilled should make you see the world mentally as you would physically were your assumption a physical fact. The spiritual man speaks to the natural man through the language of desire. The key to progress in life and to the fulfillment of dreams lies in the ready obedience to the voice. Unhesitating obedience to its voice is an immediate assumption of the wish fulfilled. To desire a state is to have it. As Pascal said, "You would not have sought me had you not already found me." Man, by assuming the feeling of the wish fulfilled and then living and acting on this conviction changes his future in harmony with his assumption. To "change his future" is the inalienable right of freedom loving individuals. There would be no progress in the world were it not for the divine discontent in man which urges him on to higher and higher levels of consciousness. I have chosen this subject so close to the hearts of us all – "Changing Your Future" – for my message next Sunday morning. I am to have the great joy of speaking for Dr. Bailes while he is vacationing. The service will be held at 10:30 at the Fox Wilshire Theater on Wilshire Boulevard near La Cienega Boulevard.

Since the right to change our future is our birthright as sons of God, let us accept its challenge and learn just how to do it. Again today, speaking of changing your future, I wish to stress the importance of a real transformation of self – not merely a slight alteration of circumstances which, in a matter of moments, will permit us to slip back into the old dissatisfied man. In your meditation, allow others to see you as they would see you were this new concept of self a concrete fact. You always seem to others the embodiment of the ideal you inspire. Therefore, in meditation, when you contemplate others, you must be seen by them mentally as you would be seen by them physically were your conception of yourself an objective fact. That is, in meditation, you imagine that they see you expressing this nobler man you desire to be. If you assume that you are what you want to be, your desire is fulfilled and, in fulfillment, all longing "to be" is neutralized. This, also, is an excellent check on yourself as to whether or not you have actually succeeded in changing self. You cannot continue desiring what has been realized. Rather, you are in a mood to give thanks for a gift received. Your desire is not something you labor to fulfill, it is recognizing something you already possess. It is assuming the feeling of being that which you desire to be.

Believing and being are one. The conceiver and his conception are one. Therefore, that which you conceive yourself to be can never be so far off as even to be near, for nearness implies separation. "If thou canst believe, all things are possible to him that believeth." Faith is the substance of things hoped for, the evidence of things not yet seen. If you assume that you are that finer, nobler one you wish to be, you will see others as they are related to your high assumption. All enlightened men wish for the good of others. If it is the good of another you seek, you must use the same controlled contemplation. In meditation, you must represent the other to yourself as already being or having the greatness you desire for him. As for yourself, your desire for another must be an intense one. It is through desire that you rise above your present sphere and the road from longing to fulfillment is shortened as you experience in imagination all that you would experience in the flesh were you or your friend the embodiment of the desire you have for yourself or him. Experience has taught me that this is the perfect way to achieve my great goals for others as well as for myself. However, my own failures would convict me were I to imply that I have completely mastered the control of my attention. I can, however, with the ancient teacher say: "This one thing I do, forgetting those things which are behind, and reaching forth unto those things which are before – I press towards the mark for the prize."

# 6

# *Truth*

I wish to ask each one of you listening to me today a question – a question which must be close to the hearts of us all concerning truth. If a man known to you as a murderer broke into your home and asked the whereabouts of your mother, would you tell him where she was? Would you tell him the truth? Would you? I venture not – I hope not. In the most mystical of the Gospels – in the Gospel of St. John we read, "Ye shall know the truth, and the truth shall make you free." Therein lies a challenge to us all, "The truth shall make you free." If you told the truth concerning your mother, would you set her free? Again, in John we read, "Sanctify them by the truth." If you gave your mother up to a murderer, would you "sanctify her?" What, then, is the truth of which the Bible so constantly speaks? The truth of the Bible is always coupled with love. The truth of the Bible is that spiritual realization of conscious life in God towards which the human soul evolves through all eternity.

Truth is an ever-increasing illumination. No one who seeks sincerely for truth need fear the outcome for every raising erstwhile truth brings into view some larger truth which it had hidden. The true seeker after truth is not a smug, critical, holier than thou person. Rather, the true seeker after truth knows the words of Zechariah to be true. "Speak ye every man the truth to his neighbor and let none of you imagine evil in your hearts against his neighbor." The seeker after truth does not judge from appearances – he sees the good, the truth in all he observes. He knows that a true judgment need not conform to the external reality to which it relates. Never are we so blind to the truth as when we see things as they seem to be. Only pictures that idealize really depict the truth. It is never superior insight but rather, purblindness that reads into the greatness of another some littleness with which it happens to be familiar.

We all know at least one petty gossip who not only imagines evil against his neighbor, but also insists upon spreading that evil far and wide. His cruel accusations are always accompanied by the statement, "It's a fact," or "I know it's the truth." How far from the truth he is. Even if it were the truth as he knows the truth, it is better not to voice it for "A truth told with bad intent beats all the lies you can invent." Such a man is not a seeker after the truth as revealed in the Bible. He seeks not truth so much as support for his own point of view. By his prejudices, he opens a door by which his enemies enter and make their own the secret places of his heart. Let us seek sincerely for the truth as Robert Browning expresses it:

*"Truth is within ourselves; it take no rise*
*From outward things, whate'er you may believe.*
*There is an immortal center in us all*
*Where truth abides in fullness.*

The truth that is within us is governed by imaginative love. Knowing this great truth, we can no longer imagine evil against any neighbor. We will imagine the best of our neighbor.

It is my belief that wherever man's attitude towards life is governed by imaginative love, there it is religious – there he worships – there he perceives the truth. I am going to speak on this subject next Sunday morning when my title will be, "Imaginative Love." At that time, I am to have the pleasure and the privilege of taking Dr. Frederick Bailes' service at the Fox Wilshire Theater on Wilshire Boulevard near La Cienega. The service will be held as Dr. Bailes always conducts it at 10:30 Sunday morning.

It is an intuitive desire of all mankind to be a finer, nobler being, to do the loving thing. But we can do the loving thing only when all we imagine is full of love for our neighbor. Then we know the truth, the truth that sets all mankind free. I believe this is a message that will aid us all in the art of living a better and finer life. Infinite love in unthinkable origin was called God, the Father. Infinite love in creative expression was called God, the Son. Infinite love in universal interpenetration, in Infinite Immanence, and in Eternal procession, was called God, the Holy Ghost. We must learn to know ourselves as Infinite Love, as good rather than evil. This is not something that we have to become; it is, rather, for us to recognize something that we are already.

The original birthplace of imagination is in love. Love is its lifeblood. Insofar as imagination retains its own life's blood, its visions are images of truth. Then it mirrors the living identity of the thing it beholds. But if imagination should deny the very power that has brought it to birth then the direst sort of horror will begin. Instead of rendering back living images of the truth, imagination will fly to love's opposite – fear and its visions will then be perverted and contorted reflections cast upon a screen of frightful fantasy. Instead of being the supremely creative power, it will become the active agent of destruction. Wherever man's attitude to life is truly imaginative, there man and God are merged in creative unity. Remember that Love is always creative, causative in every sphere from the highest to the very lowest. There never has existed thought, word or deed that was not caused by love, or by its opposite – fear of some kind, even if it were only a desire of a not very worthy aim. Love and fear are the mainspring of our mental machinery. Everything is a thought before it becomes a thing. I suggest the pursuit of a high ideal to make a fact of being become a fact of consciousness and to do this by training the imagination to realize that the only atmosphere in which we truly live and move and have our being is Infinite Love. God is Love. Love never faileth. Infinite Creative Spirit is Love. The urge that caused Infinite unconditioned consciousness to condition itself into millions of sensitive forms is Love.

Love regarded as an abstraction – apart from an object – is unthinkable. Love is not love if there is no beloved. Love only becomes thinkable in relation, in process in act. Let us recognize with Blake that, "He who will not live by love must be subdued by fear," and set ourselves the highest of ideals to love and to live by. But our highest ideals do not bless unless they come down and take on flesh. We must make results and accomplishments the crucial test of our imagination and our love, for incarnation is the only true realization. Our faithfulness must be to the sum of all the truth we know and it must be absolute. Otherwise, that truth lacks a vehicle and cannot be incarnated in us.

Our concept of ourselves determines the scenery of our lives. We are ever our own jailers. The prison doors that we thought closed are truly ajar – waiting for us to see the truth. "Man ever surrounds himself with the true image of himself," said Emerson. "Every spirit builds itself a house and beyond its house, a world, and beyond its world, a heaven. Know then the world exists for you, for you the phenomenon is perfect. What we are that only can we see. All that Adam had, all the Caesar could, you have and can do."

Adam called his house heaven and earth. Caesar called his house, Rome. You perhaps call yours a cobbler's trade, or a hundred acres of land, or a scholar's garret. Yet line for line, and point for point, your dominion is as great as theirs, though without such fine names. Build, therefore, your own world and as fast as you confirm your life to the pure idea in your mind, that will unfold its great proportions.

The truth is our secret inward reality, the cause, the meaning, the relation of our lives to all things. Let the truth carry us heavenwards, expanding our conceptions, increasing our understanding until we know the "Truth" and are made "Free."

# 7

# *Stone, Water or Wine?*

It has been my privilege and pleasure to address Dr. Frederick Bailes' Sunday audiences in the past few years. Today, I am to extend the privilege in speaking to you, his unseen audience of the radio. This will be a very practical series of talks for my subjects will be drawn largely from the Bible, the most spiritual of all books. And I am firmly convinced that whatever is most profoundly spiritual is, in reality, most directly practical. All mistakes made in Biblical interpretation come from referring statements of which the intention is spiritual and mystical, and implying principles or states to times, persons or places. In one sense, not one work of Scripture is true according to the letter. Yet, I say that every word is true; but the Scriptures are true only as He intended them that spoke them; they are true as God meant them, not as man will have them. A spiritual and symbolical interpretation alone yields truth, whilst a literal acceptation profits nothing. The Bible contains historical elements, but these are always used as picture language of great ideas.

The Gospel narrative is to be studied in order that we may know. It does not convey knowledge immediately. Getting to know is a gradual process – a progressive inner experience. God reveals Himself within us as we are able to receive Him. The deep meanings have always been recognized partially by a few, as will be found by consulting the writings of the seers of all past ages.

In assigning to the Bible its proper meaning, it is necessary to remember that as mystical Scriptures it deals primarily, not with material things or persons, but with spiritual significations. The Bible is addressed not to the outer sense or reason, but to the soul. Its object is not to give an historical account of physical life, but to exhibit the spiritual possibilities of humanity, at large, for religion is not in its nature historical and dependent upon actual sensible events, but consists in processes such as Faith and Redemption. These, being interior to all men, subsist irrespective of what any particular man has at any time done. The perennial value of the Bible is its symbolic value. There are great controversies as to what is and what is not historical in the Bible, but let us remember that if we could settle all the historical questions tomorrow, that would not give us religion, nor would it give the Bible a biding value. Everything depends upon our finding the symbolical value of the facts. A fact of past history has nothing in it for present day religion unless it stands forth as a symbol of a Reality behind itself.

The Bible is a revelation of Truth expressed in Divine symbolism. From the literal point of view, the wording may sometimes be confusing; it is the symbolism, alone, which is precious and worthy of our best efforts to elucidate. All Scripture was written from the inward mystery and not with a mystical sense put into it. The stories conceal an underlying meaning, and the task of scripture interpretation is to discover these psychological truths which are expressed in this symbolism. We, here, are not concerned with the surface meaning of the Scripture, whether it be reasonable or absurd, for in no case does it constitute the inner truth we are seeking. Throughout the centuries we have mistakenly taken personification for persons, allegory for history, the vehicle that conveyed the instruction for the instruction itself and the gross first sense for the ultimate sense intended. In most of the little things of life, this confusion is of trivial consequence. But the error which arises when you carry the confusion into questions of greater moment, such as religion, assumes gigantic proportions. For centuries, men have sought eagerly for bits of evidence which might be related to the happenings described in the Bible. While most people believe that its characters lived, no proof of their lives on earth has ever been found and may never be found. This is unimportant for the ancient teachers were not writing history, but an allegorical picture lesson of certain basic principles, which they clothed in the garb of history. The form of the various stories of the Bible is as distinct from its substance as the form of a grain of wheat is distinct from the life germ within it. As the assimilative organs of the body discriminate between food that can be built into the physical system and food that must be cast off, so do the awakened intuitive faculties discover, beneath allegory and parable, the psychological life germ, and feeding on this, they cast off the fiction which conveyed it. The Bible is the largest selling book in this country. It is probably the least read and certainly the least understood. Throughout the Bible, the symbols of stone, water and wine are used. The stones of the Bible are its literal truths. The Ten Commandments, we are told, were written on stone. The water of the Bible is the psychological meaning hidden in these literal truths of stone. "I give you living waters," that is, the inner knowledge that can make these stories a living reality in your life. The wine you must make for yourself through the wise use of this living water or psychological truth. This is an absolute necessity to the truly religious man. This is what Sir Walter Scott meant when he said, "Man's greatest education is that which he gives to himself."

On Sunday morning, I shall speak on, "Are You Stone, Water or Wine?" I shall be taking Dr. Bailes' service at 10:30 at the Fox Wilshire Theater on Wilshire Boulevard near La Cienega. When you hear this message, you may ask yourselves, "Are you stone, water or wine?" You may judge whether your understanding of the Bible is merely literal, psychological, or truly spiritual and, therefore, profoundly practical.

The Bible is, from beginning to end, all about transcending the violence which characterizes mankind's present level of being. It affirms the possibility of a development of another level of being surmounting violence. The point of view taken is that the goal of man is this inner development, which is the only real psychology. To take the Bible away from its central idea of rebirth, which means an inner evolution and implies the existence of a higher level, is to understand nothing of its real meaning. The Word of God, that is, the psychological teaching in the Bible, is to make a man different, first in thought and then in being, so that he becomes a new man or is born again.

Whenever an entirely new attitude enters into a person's life, psychological rebirth to some extent has occurred. Man wants to be better, not different. The Bible speaks, not of being better, but of another man, a man reborn. "Except a man be born again, he cannot see the Kingdom of God... Except a man be born of water and the spirit, he cannot enter into the Kingdom of God. Marvel not that I said unto thee, ye must be born again." (John 3.) The Ten Commandments were written on tablets of stone for those incapable of seeing any deeper meaning. Stone represents the most external and literal form of spiritual truth, and water refers to another way of understanding the same truth. Wine or spirit is the highest form of understanding it.

"Such as men themselves are, such will God appear to them to be," wrote John Smith, the Cambridge Platonist. "The God of the moralist is before all things a great judge and schoolmaster; the God of Science is impersonal and inflexible Vital Law; the God of the savage is the kind of chief he would be himself if he had the opportunity." No man's conduct will be higher than his conception of God, and his conception of God is determined by the kind of man he, himself, is. "For such as men themselves are, such will God appear to them to be," and what is true of man's concept of God is equally true of man's concept of God's Word, the Bible. It will be to him what he is to himself.

*"God is God from the creation,*
*Truth alone is man's salvation;*
*But the God that now you worship*
*Soon shall be your God no more*
*For the soul in its unfolding*

*Evermore its thoughts remolding,*
*Learns more truly in its progress*
*How to love and to adore."*

# 8

# *Feeling is the Secret*

Recently, I asked a very successful businessman his formula for success. He laughed and was a little embarrassed. Then he replied, "I guess it's just because I can't conceive of failure. It's nothing that I think about much. It's more a feeling that I have." His statement coincided completely with my own beliefs and experiments. We can think about something forever and never see it in our world, but once let us feel its reality, and we are bound to encounter it. The more intensely we feel, the sooner we will encounter it. We all regard feelings far too much as effects, and not sufficiently as causes of the events of the day. Feeling is not only the result of our conditions of life, it is also the creator of those conditions. We say we are happy because we are well, not realizing that the process will work equally well in the reverse direction. We are well because we are happy. We are all far too undisciplined in our feelings. To be joyful for another is to bless ourselves as well as him. To be angry with another is to punish ourselves for his fault. The distressed mind stays at home though the body travels to the ends of the earth, while the happy mind travels though the body remains at home.

Feeling is the secret of successful prayer, for in prayer, we feel ourselves into the situation of the answered prayer and, then, we live and act upon that conviction. Feeling after Him, as the Bible suggests, is a gradual unfolding of the soul's hidden capacities. Feeling yields in importance to no other. It is the ferment without which no creation is possible. All forms of creative imagination imply elements of feeling. All emotional dispositions whatever may influence the creative imagination. Feeling after Him has no finality. It is an acquisition, increasing in proportion to receptivity, which has not and never will have finality. An idea which is only an idea produces nothing and does nothing. It acts only if it is felt, if it is accompanied by effective feeling. Somewhere within the soul there is a mood which, if found, means wealth, health, happiness to us. The creative desire is innate in man. His whole happiness is involved in this impulse to create. Because men do not perfectly "feel," the results of their prayers are unsure, when they might be perfectly sure. We read in Proverbs, "A merry heart doeth good like a medicine but a broken spirit drieth the bones." Orchestral hearts burn in the oil of the lamp of the king. The spirit sings unto the Lord a new song. All true prayer wears a glad countenance; the good are anointed with the oil of gladness above their fellows. Let us, then, watch our feelings, our reactions to the day's events. And let us guard our feelings even more zealously in the act of prayer, for prayer is the true creative state. Dignity indicates that man hears the greater music of life, and moves to the tempo of its deeper meaning. If we did nothing but imagine and feel the lovely, the world's reform would, at once, be accomplished. Many of the stories of the Bible deal exclusively with the power of imagination and feeling. "Feeling after Him" is the cry of the truth seeker. Only imagination and feeling can restore the Eden from which experience has driven us. Feeling and imagination are the senses by which we perceive the beyond. Where knowledge ends, they begin. Every noble feeling of man is the opening for him of some door to the divine world. Let us measure men, not by the height of their cities, but by the magnificence of their imaginations and feelings. Let us turn our thought up to Heaven and mix our imagination with the angels. The world that moves us is the one we imagine, not the world that surrounds us. In the imagination lie the unexplored continents, and man's great future adventure. This consciousness of non-finality in "feeling after God" has been the experience of all earnest God-ward feelers. They realize that their conception of the Infinite has constantly deepened and expanded with experience. Those who endeavor to think out the meaning of the experience and to coordinate it with the rest of our knowledge, are the philosophic mystics; those who try to develop the faculty in themselves, and to deepen the experience are the practical or experimental mystics. Some, and among them the greatest, have tried to do both. Religion begins in subjective experience. Religion is what a man does with his solitude, for in solitude we are compelled to subjective experience.

It is of the Religious Attitude that I shall speak next Sunday morning. This will be the last Sunday morning I shall take the service for Dr. Bailes this season. The service is held at 10:30 at the Fox Wilshire Theater on Wilshire Boulevard, near La Cienega. A True Religious Attitude is man's salvation. God never changes; it is we who are changing; our spiritual eyes are ever getting keener; and this enlargement of truth will bring us an ever-increasing inner peace.

The best defense against the deceptive assault upon our mental and moral eyesight is the spiritual eye or the Eye of God. In other words, a spiritual ideal that cannot be changed by circumstance, a code of personal honor and integrity in ourselves and good will and love to others. "Not what thou art, nor what thou hast been, beholdeth God with his merciful eyes, but that thou wouldst be." Through the veins of the humblest man on earth runs the royal blood of being. Therefore, let us look at man through the eyes of imaginative love which is really seeing with the Eye of God. Under the influence of the Eye of God, the ideal rises up out of the actual as water is etherealized by the sun into the imagery cloudland. Things altogether distant are present to the spiritual eye. The Eye of God makes the future dream a present fact. Not four months to harvest – look again, If we persist in this seeing, one day we will arise with the distance in our eyes, and all the staying, stagnant nearby will suddenly be of no importance. We will brush it aside as we pass on to our far-seen objective. The man who really finds himself cannot do otherwise than let himself be guided by love. He is of too pure eyes to behold iniquity. Our ability to help others will be in proportion to our ability to control and help ourselves. The day a man achieves victory over himself, history will discover that to have been a victory over his enemy. The healing touch is in an attitude, and one day man will discover that one governs souls only with serenity. The mighty surrenders itself fully only to the most gentle.

Recognizing the power of feeling, let us pay strict attention to our moods and attitudes. Every stage of man's progress is made through the exercise of his imagination and feeling. By creating an "ideal" within our mental sphere we can feel ourselves into this "ideal image" till we become one and the same with it, absorbing its qualities into the very core of our being. The solitary or captive can, by the intensity of his imagination and feeling, effect myriads so that he can act through many men and speak through many voices. Extend your feelers, trust your touch, participate in all flights of your imaginations and be not afraid of your own sensitivities. The best way to feel another's good is to be more intensely aware of it. Be like my friend and have "more of a feeling" for the health, the wealth, the happiness you desire. Ideas do not bless unless they descend from Heaven and take flesh. Make results or accomplishments the crucial test of true imagination. As you observe these results, you will determine to fill your images with love and to walk in a high and noble mood for you will know with the poet:

*"That which ye sow ye reap.*
*See yonder fields*
*The sesamum was sesamum, the corn*
*Was corn. The Silence and the Darkness knew*
*So is man's fate born."*

9

# *Affirm the Reality of Our Own Greatness*

In the creation of a new way of life, we must begin at the beginning, with our own individual regeneration. The formation of organizations, political bodies, religious bodies, social bodies is not enough. The trouble we see goes deeper than we perceive. The essential revolution must happen within ourselves. Everything depends on our attitude towards ourself – that which we will not affirm within ourself can never develop in our world. This is the religion by which we live, for religion begins in subjective experience, like charity, it begins at home. "Be ye transformed by the renewing of your mind" is the ancient formula and there is no other. Everything depends upon man's attitude toward himself. That which he cannot or will not claim as true of himself can never evolve in his world. Man is constantly looking about his world and asking, "What's to be done? What will happen?" when he should ask himself "Who am I? What is my concept of myself?" If we wish to see the world a finer, greater place, we must affirm the reality of a finer, greater being within ourselves. It is the ultimate purpose of my teaching to point the road to this consummation. I am trying to show you how the inner man must readjust himself – what must be the new premise of his life, in order that he may lose his soul on the level he now knows and find it again on the high level he seeks.

It is impossible for man to see other than the contents of his own consciousness, for nothing has existence for us save through the consciousness we have of it. The ideal man is always seeking a new incarnation but unless we, ourselves, offer him human parentage, he is incapable of birth. We are the means whereby the redemption of nature from the law of cruelty is to be effected. The great purpose of consciousness is to effect this redemption. If we decline the burden and point to natural law as giving us conclusive proof that redemption of the world by imaginative love is something that can never come about, we simply nullify the purpose of our lives through want of faith. We reject the means, the only means, whereby this process of redemption must be effected.

The only test of religion worth making is whether it is trueborn – whether it springs from the deepest conviction of the individual, whether it is the fruit of inner experience. No religion is worthy of a man unless it gives him a deep and abiding sense that all is well, quite irrespective of what happens to him personally. The methods of mental and of spiritual knowledge are entirely different, for we know a thing mentally by looking at it from the outside, by comparing it with other things by analyzing and defining it. Whitehead has defined religion as that which a man does with his solitude. I should like to add, I believe it is what a man is in his solitude. In our solitude we are driven to subjective experience. It is, then, that we should imagine ourselves to be the ideal man we desire to see embodied in the world. If, in our solitude, we experience in our imagination what we would experience in reality had we achieved our goal, we will in time, become transformed into the image of our ideal. "Be renewed in the spirit of your mind – put on the new man – speak every man truth with his neighbor." The process of making a "Fact of being a fact of consciousness" is by the "renewing of our mind." We are told to change our thinking. But we can't change our thought unless we change our ideas. Our thoughts are the natural outpouring of our ideas, and our innermost ideas are the man himself. The end of longing is always to be – not to do. Be still and know

"I am that which I desire." Strive always after being. External reforms are useless if your heart is not reformed. Heaven is entered not by curbing our passions; but rather, by cultivating our virtues. An old idea is not fickly forgotten, it is crowded out by new ideas. It disappears when a wholly new and absorbing idea occupies our attention. Old habits of thinking and feeling – like dead oak leaves – hang on till they are pushed off by new ones. Creativeness is basically a deeper receptiveness, a keener susceptibility. The future dream must become a present fact in the mind of anyone who would alter his life. Every great out-picturing is preceded by a period of profound absorption. When that absorption is filled with our highest ideal, – when we become that ideal – then we see it manifest in our world and we realize that the present does not recede into the past, but advances into the future. This is essentially how we change our future. A "now" which is "elsewhere" has for us no absolute meaning. We only recognize "now" when it is at the same time "here." When we feel ourselves into the desired state "here" and "now" we have truly changed our future. It is this "Changing Your Future" which I hope to explain to you fully next Sunday morning when I am speaking for Dr. Bailes at 10:30 at the Fox Wilshire Theater on Wilshire Boulevard near La Cienega. It is my purpose to stir you to a higher concept of yourself and to explain so clearly the method by which you can achieve this concept that each one of you will leave the service on Sunday morning a transformed being.

Discouraged people are sorely in need of the inspiration of great principles. We must get back to first principles if we are to speak with a voice that will kindle the imagination and rouse the spirit. Again, I must repeat, in the creation of a new way of life, we must begin at the very beginning with our own individual regeneration. Man's chief delusion is his conviction that he can do anything. Everyone thinks he can do – everyone wants to do and all ask, "What to do?" What to do? It is impossible to do anything. One must be. It is hard for us to accept the fact that "We, of ourselves, do nothing." It is especially difficult because it is the truth and the truth is always difficult for man to accept. But, actually, nobody can do anything. Everything happens – all that befalls man – all that is done by him – all that comes from him – all this happens, and it happens in exactly the same way that rain falls – as a result of a change in the temperature in the higher regions of the atmosphere. This is a challenge to us all. What concept are we holding of ourselves in the higher regions of our soul?

Everything depends upon man's attitude towards himself. That which he will not affirm as true within himself can never develop in his world. A change of concept of self is the right adjustment – the new relationship between the surface and the depth of man. Deepening is, in principle, always possible, for the ultimate depth lives in everyone, and it is only a question of becoming conscious of it. Life demands of us the willingness to die and to be born again. This is not meant that we die in the flesh. We die in the spirit of the old man to become the new man, then we see the new man in the flesh. "Subjection to the will of God" is an old phrase for it and there is, I believe, no new one that is better. In that self-committal to the ideal we desire to express, all conflict is dispersed and we are transformed into the image of the ideal in whom we rest. We are told that the man without a wedding garment reaches the Kingdom by cleverly pretending. He does not believe internally what he practices externally. He appears good, kind, charitable. He uses the right words, but inwardly he believes nothing. Coming into the strong light of those far more conscious than himself, he ceases to deceive. A wedding garment signifies a desire for union. He has no desire to unite with what he teaches, even if what he teaches is the truth. Therefore, he has no wedding garment. When we are united with the truth, then we will put off the old nature and be renewed in the spirit of our mind.

Truth will strip the clever pretenders of their false aristocracy. Truth, in its turn, will be conquered and governed by the aristocracy of goodness, the only unconquerable thing in the world.

3

# *Feeling is the Secret*

# *Foreword*

This book is concerned with the art of realizing your desire. It gives you an account of the mechanism used in the production of the visible world. It is a small book but not slight. There is a treasure in it, a clearly defined road to the realization of your dreams.

Were it possible to carry conviction to another by means of reasoned arguments and detailed instances, this book would be many times its size. It is seldom possible, however, to do so by means of written statements or arguments since to the suspended judgment it always seems plausible to say that the author was dishonest or deluded, and, therefore, his evidence was tainted.

Consequently, I have purposely omitted all arguments and testimonials, and simply challenge the open-minded reader to practice the law of consciousness as revealed in this book. Personal success will prove far more convincing than all the books that could be written on the subject.

**–Neville Goddard**

1

# *Law and Its Operation*

The world, and all within it, is man's conditioned consciousness objectified. Consciousness is the cause as well as the substance of the entire world. So it is to consciousness that we must turn if we would discover the secret of creation.

Knowledge of the law of consciousness and the method of operating this law will enable you to accomplish all you desire in life. Armed with a working knowledge of this law, you can build and maintain an ideal world.

Consciousness is the one and only reality, not figuratively but actually. This reality may for the sake of clarity be likened unto a stream which is divided into two parts, the conscious and the subconscious. In order to intelligently operate the law of consciousness, it is necessary to understand the relationship between the conscious and the subconscious. The conscious is personal and selective; the subconscious is impersonal and non-selective. The conscious is the realm of effect; the subconscious is the realm of cause. These two aspects are the male and female divisions of consciousness. The conscious is male; the subconscious is female.

The conscious generates ideas and impresses these ideas on the subconscious; the subconscious receives ideas and gives form and expression to them.

By this law first conceiving an idea and then impressing the idea conceived on the subconscious – all things evolve out of consciousness; and without this sequence, there is not anything made that is made. The conscious impresses the subconscious, while the subconscious expresses all that is impressed upon it.

The subconscious does not originate ideas, but accepts as true those which the conscious mind feels to be true and, in a way known only to it-self, objectifies the accepted ideas. Therefore, through his power to imagine and feel and his freedom to choose the idea he will entertain, man has control over creation. Control of the subconscious is accomplished through control of your ideas and feelings.

The mechanism of creation is hidden in the very depth of the subconscious, the female aspect or womb of creation. The subconscious transcends reason and is independent of induction. It contemplates a feeling as a fact existing within itself and on this assumption proceeds to give expression to it. The creative process begins with an idea and its cycle runs its course as a feeling and ends in a volition to act.

Ideas are impressed on the subconscious through the medium of feeling. No idea can be impressed on the subconscious until it is felt, but once felt – be it good, bad or indifferent – it must be expressed. Feeling is the one and only medium through which ideas are conveyed to the subconscious. Therefore, the man who does not control his feeling may easily impress the subconscious with undesirable states. By control of feeling is not meant restraint or suppression of your feeling, but rather the disciplining of self to imagine and entertain only such feeling as contributes to your happiness. Control of your feeling is all important to a full and happy life. Never entertain an undesirable feeling, nor think sympathetically about wrong in any shape or form. Do not dwell on the imperfection of yourself or others. To do so is to impress the subconscious with these limitations. What you do not want done unto you, do not feel that it is done unto you or another. This is the whole law of a full and happy life. Everything else is commentary.

Every feeling makes a subconscious impression and, unless it is counteracted by a more powerful feeling of an opposite nature, must be expressed. The dominant of two feelings is the one expressed. I am healthy is a stronger feeling than I will be healthy. To feel I will be is to confess I am not; I am is stronger than I am not. What you feel you are always dominates what you feel you would like to be; therefore, to be realized, the wish must be felt as a state that is rather than a state that is not. Sensation precedes manifestation and is the foundation upon which all manifestation rests. Be careful of your moods and feelings, for there is an unbroken connection between your feelings and your visible world. Your body is an emotional filter and bears the unmistakable marks of your prevalent emotions. Emotional disturbances, especially suppressed emotions, are the causes of all disease. To feel intensely about a wrong with-out voicing or expressing that feeling is the beginning of disease – disease in both body and environment. Do not entertain the feeling of regret or failure for frustration or detachment from your objective results in disease.

Think feelingly only of the state you desire to realize. Feeling the reality of the state sought and living and acting on that conviction is the way of all seeming miracles. All changes of expression are brought about through a change of feeling. A change of feeling is a change of destiny. All creation occurs in the domain of the subconscious. What you must acquire, then, is a reflective control of the operation of the subconscious, that is, control of your ideas and feelings.

Chance or accident is not responsible for the things that happen to you, nor is predestined fate the author of your fortune or misfortune. Your subconscious impressions determine the conditions of your world. The subconscious is not selective; it is impersonal and no respecter of persons [Acts 10:34; Romans 2:11]. The subconscious is not concerned with the truth or falsity of your feeling. It always accepts as true that which you feel to be true. Feeling is the assent of the subconscious to the truth of that which is declared to be true. Because of this quality of the subconscious there is nothing impossible to man. Whatever the mind of man can conceive and feel as true, the subconscious can and must objectify.

Your feelings create the pattern from which your world is fashioned, and a change of feeling is a change of pattern.

The subconscious never fails to express that which has been impressed upon it. The moment it receives an impression, it begins to work out the ways of its expression. It accepts the feeling impressed upon it, you're feeling, as a fact existing within itself and immediately sets about to produce in the outer or objective world the exact likeness of that feeling. The subconscious never alters the accepted beliefs of man. It out-pictures them to the last detail whether or not they are beneficial.

To impress the subconscious with the desirable state, you must assume the feeling that would be yours had you already realized your wish. In defining your objective, you must be concerned only with the objective itself. The manner of expression or the difficulties involved are not to be considered by you. To think feelingly on any state impresses it on the sub-conscious. Therefore, if you dwell on difficulties, barriers or delay, the subconscious, by its very non-selective nature, accepts the feeling of difficulties and obstacles as your request and proceeds to produce them in your outer world. The subconscious is the womb of creation. It receives the idea unto itself through the feelings of man. It never changes the idea received, but always gives it form. Hence the subconscious out-pictures the idea in the image and likeness of the feeling received. To feel a state as hopeless or impossible is to impress the subconscious with the idea of failure.

Although the subconscious faithfully serves man, it must not be inferred that the relation is that of a servant to a master as was anciently conceived. The ancient prophets called it the slave and servant of man. St. Paul personified it as a "woman" and said: "The woman should be subject to man in everything" [Ephesians 5:24; also, 1Corinthians 14:34, Ephesians 5:22, Colossians 3:18, 1Peter 3:1]. The subconscious does serve man and faithfully gives form to his feelings. However, the subconscious has a distinct distaste for compulsion and responds to persuasion rather than to command; consequently, it resembles the beloved wife more than the servant.

"The husband is head of the wife," Ephesians 5[:23], may not be true of man and woman in their earthly relationship, but it is true of the conscious and the subconscious, or the male and female aspects of consciousness. The mystery to which Paul referred when he wrote, "This is a great mystery [5:32]… He that loveth his wife loveth himself [5:28]… And they two shall be one flesh [5:31]", is simply the mystery of consciousness. Consciousness is really one and undivided but for creation's sake it appears to be divided into two.

The conscious (objective) or male aspect truly is the head and dominates the subconscious (subjective) or female aspect. However, this leadership is not that of the tyrant, but of the lover. So, by assuming the feeling that would be yours were you already in possession of your objective, the sub-conscious is moved to build the exact likeness of your assumption. Your desires are not subconsciously accepted until you assume the feeling of their reality, for only through feeling is an idea subconsciously accepted and only through this subconscious acceptance is it ever expressed.

It is easier to ascribe your feeling to events in the world than to admit that the conditions of the world reflect your feeling. However, it is eternally true that the outside mirrors the inside. "As within, so without" ["As above, so below; as below, so above; as within, so without; as without, so within", "Correspondence", the second of The Seven Principles of Hermes Trismegistus]. "A man can receive nothing unless it is given him from heaven" [John 3:27] and "The kingdom of heaven is within you" [Luke17:21]. Nothing comes from without; all things come from within – from the subconscious. It is impossible for you to see other than the con-tents of your consciousness. Your world in its every detail is your consciousness objectified. Objective states bear witness of subconscious impressions. A change of impression results in a change of expression.

The subconscious accepts as true that which you feel as true, and because creation is the result of subconscious impressions, you, by your feeling, determine creation. You are already that which you want to be, and your refusal to believe this is the only reason you do not see it. To seek on the outside for that which you do not feel you are is to seek in vain, for we never find that which we want; we find only that which we are. In short, you express and have only that which you are conscious of being or possessing. "To him that hath it is given" [Matthew 13:12; 25:29; Mark 4:25; Luke 8:18; 19:26]. Denying the evidence of the senses and appropriating the feeling of the wish fulfilled is the way to the realization of your desire.

Mastery of self-control of your thoughts and feelings is your highest achievement. However, until perfect self-control is attained, so that, in spite of appearances, you feel all that you want to feel, use sleep and prayer to aid you in realizing your desired states. These are the two gate-ways into the subconscious.

2

# *Sleep*

Sleep, the life that occupies one- third of our stay on earth, is the natural door into the subconscious. So it is with sleep that we are now concerned. The conscious two-thirds of our life on earth is measured by the degree of attention we give sleep. Our understanding of and delight in what sleep has to bestow will cause us, night after night, to set out for it as though we were keeping an appointment with a lover.

"In a dream, in a vision of the night, when deep sleep falleth upon men, in slumbering upon the bed; then he openeth the ears of men and sealeth their instruction", Job 33. It is in sleep and in prayer, a state akin to sleep, that man enters the subconscious to make his impressions and receive his instructions. In these states the conscious and subconscious are creatively joined. The male and female become one flesh. Sleep is the time when the male or conscious mind turns from the world of sense to seek its lover or subconscious self. The subconscious - unlike the woman of the world who marries her husband to change him – has no desire to change the conscious, waking state, but loves it as it is and faithfully reproduces its likeness in the outer world of form. The conditions and events of your life are your children formed from the molds of your subconscious impressions in sleep. They are made in the image and likeness of your innermost feeling that they may reveal you to yourself.

"As in heaven, so on earth" [Matthew 6:10; Luke 11:2]. As in the subconscious, soon earth. Whatever you have in consciousness as you go to sleep is the measure of your expression in the waking two-thirds of your life on earth. Nothing stops you from realizing your objective save your failure to feel that you are already that which you wish to be, or that you are already in possession of the thing sought. Your subconscious gives form to your desires only when you feel your wish fulfilled.

The unconsciousness of sleep is the normal state of the subconscious. Be-cause all things come from within yourself, and your conception of yourself determines that which comes, you should always feel the wish fulfilled before you drop off to sleep. You never draw out of the deep of yourself that which you want; you always draw that which you are, and you are that which you feel yourself to be as well as that which you feel as true of others.

To be realized, then, the wish must be resolved into the feeling of being or having or witnessing the state sought. This is accomplished by assuming the feeling of the wish fulfilled. The feeling which comes in response to the question "How would I feel were my wish realized?" is the feeling which should monopolize and immobilize your attention as you relax into sleep. You must be in the consciousness of being or having that which you want to be or to have before you drop off to sleep.

Once asleep, man has no freedom of choice. His entire slumber is dominated by his last waking concept of self. It follows, therefore, that he should always assume the feeling of accomplishment and satisfaction be-fore here tires in sleep, "Come before me with singing and thanksgiving" [Psalm95:2], "Enter into his gates with thanksgiving and into his courts with praise" [Psalm 100:4]. Your mood prior to sleep defines your state of consciousness as you enter into the presence of your everlasting lover, the subconscious. She sees you exactly as you feel yourself to be. If, as you prepare for sleep, you assume and maintain the consciousness of success by feeling "I am successful", you must be successful. Lie flat on your back with your head on a level with your body. Feel as you would were you in possession of your wish and quietly relax into unconsciousness.

"He that keepeth Israel shall neither slumber nor sleep" [Psalm 121:4]. Nevertheless "He giveth his beloved sleep" [Psalm 127:2]. The subconscious never sleeps. Sleep is the door through which the conscious, waking mind passes to be creatively joined to the subconscious.

Sleep conceals the creative act, while the objective world reveals it. In sleep, man impresses the subconscious with his conception of himself. What more beautiful description of this romance of the conscious and sub-conscious is there than that told in the "Song of Solomon": "By night on my bed I sought him whom my soul loveth [3:1]... I found him whom my soul loveth; I held him and I not let him go, until I had brought him into my mother's house, and into the chamber of her that conceived me" [3:4].

Preparing to sleep, you feel yourself into the state of the answered wish, and then relax into unconsciousness. Your realized wish is he whom you seek. By night, on your bed, you seek the feeling of the wish fulfilled that you may take it with you into the chamber of her that conceived you, into sleep or the subconscious which gave you form, that this wish also may be given expression. This is the way to discover and conduct your wishes into the subconscious. Feel yourself in the state of the realized wish and quietly drop off to sleep.

Night after night, you should assume the feeling of being, having and witnessing that which you seek to be, possess and see manifested. Never go to sleep feeling discouraged or dissatisfied. Never sleep in the consciousness of failure. Your subconscious, whose natural state is sleep, sees you as you believe yourself to be, and whether it be good, bad or indifferent, the subconscious will faithfully embody your belief. As you feel so do you impress her; and she, the perfect lover, gives form to these impressions and out-pictures them as the children of her beloved.

"Thou art all fair, my love; there is no spot in the" [Song of Solomon 4:7] is the attitude of mind to adopt before dropping off to sleep. Disregard appearances and feel that things are as you wish them to be, for

"He calleth things that are not seen as though they were, and the unseen be-comes seen"[Approx., Romans 4:17]. To assume the feeling of satisfaction is to call conditions into being which will mirror satisfaction. "Signs follow, they do not precede". Proof that you are will follow the consciousness that you are; it will not precede it. You are an eternal dreamer dreaming non-eternal dreams. Your dreams take form as you assume the feeling of their reality. Do not limit yourself to the past. Knowing that nothing is impossible to consciousness, begin to imagine states beyond the experiences of the past. Whatever the mind of man can imagine, man can realize. All objective (visible) states were first subjective (invisible) states, and you called them into visible by assuming the feeling of their reality. The creative process is first imagining and then believing the state imagined. Always imagine and expect the best.

The world cannot change until you change your conception of it. "As within, so without". Nations, as well as people, are only what you believe them to be. No matter what the problem is, no matter where it is, no matter whom it concerns, you have no one to change but yourself, and you have neither opponent nor helper in bringing about the change within yourself. You have nothing to do but convince yourself of the truth of that which you desire to see manifested. As soon as you succeed in convincing yourself of the reality of the state sought, results follow to confirm your fixed belief. You never suggest to another the state which you desire to see him express; instead, you convince yourself that he is already that which you desire him to be.

Realization of your wish is accomplished by assuming the feeling of the wish fulfilled. You cannot fail unless you fail to convince yourself of the reality of your wish. A change of belief is confirmed by a change of expression. Every night, as you drop off to sleep, feel satisfied and spotless, for your subjective lover always forms the objective world in the image and likeness of your conception of it, the conception defined by your feeling.

The waking two-thirds of your life on earth ever corroborates or bears witness to your subconscious impressions. The actions and events of the day are effects; they are not causes. Free will is only freedom of choice.

"Choose ye this day whom ye shall serve" [Joshua 24:15] is your freedom to choose the kind of mood you assume; but the expression of the mood is the secret of the subconscious. The subconscious receives impressions only through the feelings of man and, in a way known only to itself, gives these impressions form and expression. The actions of man are deter-mined by his subconscious impressions. His illusion of free will, his belief in freedom of action, is but ignorance of the causes which make him act. He thinks himself free because he has forgotten the link between himself and the event.

Man awake is under compulsion to express his subconscious impressions. If in the past he unwisely impressed himself, then let him begin to change his thought and feeling, for only as he does so will the change his world.

Do not waste one moment in regret, for to think feelingly of the mistakes of the past is to reinfect yourself. "Let the dead bury the dead" [Matthew 8:22; Luke 9:60]. Turn from appearances and assume the feeling that would be yours were you already the one you wish to be.

Feeling a state produces that state. The part you play on the world's stage is determined by your conception of yourself. By feeling your wish fulfilled and quietly relaxing into sleep, you cast yourself in a star role to be played on earth tomorrow, and, while asleep, you are rehearsed and instructed in your part.

The acceptance of the end automatically wills the means of realization. Make no mistake about this. If, as you prepare for sleep, you do not consciously feel yourself into the state of the answered wish, then you will take with you into the chamber of her who conceived you the sum total of the reactions and feelings of the waking day; and while asleep, you will be instructed in the manner in which they will be expressed tomorrow. You will rise believing that you are a free agent, not realizing that every action and event of the day is predetermined by your concept of self as you fell asleep. Your only freedom, then, is your freedom of reaction. You are free to choose how you feel and react to the day's drama, but the drama –

the actions, events and circumstances of the day – have already been determined.

Unless you consciously and purposely define the attitude of mind with which you go to sleep, you unconsciously go to sleep in the composite attitude of mind made up of all feelings and reactions of the day. Every reaction makes a subconscious impression and, unless counteracted by an opposite and more dominant feeling, is the cause of future action.

Ideas enveloped in feeling are creative actions. Use your divine right wisely. Through your ability to think and feel, you have dominion over all creation.

While you are awake, you are a gardener selecting seed for your garden, but "Except a corn of wheat fall into the ground and die, it abideth alone; but if it die, it bringeth forth much fruit" [John 12:24]. Your conception of yourself as you fall asleep is the seed you drop into the ground of the subconscious. Dropping off to sleep feeling satisfied and happy compels conditions and events to appear in your world which confirm these attitudes of mind.

Sleep is the door into heaven. What you take in as a feeling you bring out as a condition, action, or object in space. So sleep in the feeling of the wish fulfilled. "As in consciousness, so on earth."

# 3

# *Prayer*

Prayer, like sleep, is also an entrance into the subconscious. "When you pray, enter into your closet, and when you have shut your door, pray to your Father which is in secret and your Father which is in secret shall reward you openly" [Matthew 6:6].

Prayer is an illusion of sleep which diminishes the impression of the outer world and renders the mind more receptive to suggestion from within. The mind in prayer is in a state of relaxation and receptivity akin to the feeling attained just before dropping off to sleep.

Prayer is not so much what you ask for, as how you prepare for its reception. "Whatsoever things ye desire, when ye pray believe that you have received them, and ye shall have them" [Mark 11:24]. The only condition required is that you believe that your prayers are already realized.

Your prayer must be answered if you assume the feeling that would be yours were you already in possession of your objective. The moment you accept the wish as an accomplished fact, the subconscious finds means for its realization. To pray successfully then, you must yield to the wish, that is, feel the wish fulfilled.

The perfectly disciplined man is always in tune with the wish as an accomplished fact. He knows that consciousness is the one and only reality, that ideas and feelings are facts of consciousness and are as real as objects in space; therefore he never entertains a feeling which does not contribute to his happiness, for feelings are the causes of the actions and circumstances of his life. On the other hand, the undisciplined man finds it difficult to believe that which is denied by the senses and usually accepts or rejects solely on appearances of the senses. Because of this tendency to rely on the evidence of the senses, it is necessary to shut them out before starting to pray, before attempting to feel that which they deny. Whenever you are in the state of mind "I should like to, but I cannot", the harder you try, the less you are able to yield to the wish. You never attract that which you want, but always attract that which you are conscious of being.

Prayer is the art of assuming the feeling of being and having that which you want. When the senses confirm the absence of your wish, all conscious effort to counteract this suggestion is futile and tends to intensify the suggestion.

Prayer is the art of yielding to the wish and not the forcing of the wish. Whenever your feeling is in conflict with your wish, feeling will be the victor. The dominant feeling invariably expresses itself. Prayer must be without effort. In attempting to fix an attitude of mind which is denied by the senses, effort is fatal.

To yield successfully to the wish as an accomplished fact, you must create a passive state, a kind of reverie or meditative reflection similar to the feeling which precedes sleep. In such a relaxed state, the mind is turned from the objective world and easily senses the reality of a subjective state. It is a state in which you are conscious and quite able to move or open your eyes but have no desire to do so. An easy way to create this passive state is to relax in a comfortable chair or on a bed. If on a bed, lie flat on your back with your head on a level with your body, close the eyes and imagine that you are sleepy. Feel – I am sleepy, so sleepy, so very sleepy. In a little while, a faraway feeling accompanied by a general lassitude and loss of all desire to move envelops you. You feel a pleasant, comfortable rest and not inclined to alter your position, although under other circumstances you would not be at all comfortable. When this passive state is reached, imagine that you have realized your wish – not how it was realized, but simply the wish fulfilled. Imagine in picture form what you desire to achieve in life; then feel yourself as having already achieved it. Thoughts produce tiny little speech movements which may be heard in the passive state of prayer as pronouncements from without. However, this degree of passivity is not essential to the realization of your prayers. All that is necessary is to create a passive state and feel the wish fulfilled.

All you can possibly need or desire is already yours. You need no helper to give it to you; it is yours now. Call your desires into being by imagining and feeling your wish fulfilled. As the end is accepted, you become totally indifferent as to possible failure, for acceptance of the end wills the means to that end. When you emerge from the moment of prayer, it is as though you were shown the happy and successful end of a play although you were not shown how that end was achieved. However, having witnessed the end, regardless of any anticlimactic sequence, you remain calm and secure in the knowledge that the end has been perfectly defined.

# 4

# *Spirit – Feeling*

"Not by might, nor by power, but by my spirit, saith the Lord of hosts" [Zechariah 4:6]. Get into the spirit of the state desired by assuming the feeling that would be yours were you already the one you want to be. As you capture the feeling of the state sought, you are relieved of all effort to make it so, for it is already so. There is a definite feeling associated with every idea in the mind of man. Capture the feeling associated with your realized wish by assuming the feeling that would be yours were you already in possession of the thing you desire, and your wish will objectify itself.

Faith is feeling, "According to your faith (feeling) be it unto you" [Matthew 9:29]. You never attract that which you want, but always that which you are. As a man is, so does he see. "To him that hath it shall be given and to him that hath not it shall be taken away…" [Matthew 13:12; 25:29; Mark 4:25;Luke 8:18; 19:26]. That which you feel yourself to be you are, and you are given that which you are. So assume the feeling that would be yours were you already in possession of your wish, and your wish must be realized. "So God created man in his own image, in the image of God created he him" [Genesis 1:27]. "Let this mind be in you which was also in Christ Jesus, who being in the form of God, thought it not robbery to be equal with God" [Philippians 2:5,6]. You are that which you believe your-self to be. Instead of believing in God or in Jesus – believe you are

God or you are Jesus. "He that believeth on Me, the works that I do shall he do also" [John14:12] should be "He that believes as I believe the works that I do shall he do also". Jesus found it not strange to do the works of God, because He believed Himself to be God. "I and My Father are one" [John 10:30]. It is natural to do the works of the one you believe yourself to be. So live in the feeling of being the one you want to be and that you shall be.

When a man believes in the value of the advice given him and applies it, he establishes within himself the reality of success.

4

# The Power of Awareness

*To*

Arthur and his beloved Verne
whose awareness brought this book into being.

# 1

# *I Am*

> "All things when they are admitted are made manifest by the light: for everything that is made manifest is light."
>
> **Ephesians 5:13**

The "Light" is consciousness. Consciousness is *one*, manifesting in legions of forms or levels of consciousness. There is no one that is not *all* that is, for consciousness, though expressed in an infinite series of levels, is not divisional. There is no real separation or gap in consciousness. 'I AM' cannot be divided. I may conceive myself to be a rich man, a poor man, a beggar man or a thief, but the center of my being remains the same regardless of the concept I hold of myself. At the center of manifestation there is only one 'I AM' manifesting in legions of forms or concepts of itself and "I am that I am".

'I AM' is the selfdefinition of the absolute, the foundation on which everything rests. 'I AM' is the first cause-substance. 'I AM' is the selfdefinition of God.

"I AM hath sent me unto you."

"I AM THAT I AM."

"Be still and know that I AM God."

'I AM' is a feeling of permanent awareness. The very center of consciousness is the feeling of 'I AM' I may forget *who* I am, *where* I am, *what* I am but I cannot forget that I AM. The awareness of *being* remains, regardless of the degree of forgetfulness of who, where and what I am.

'I AM' is that which, amid unnumbered forms, is ever the same. This great discovery of cause reveals that, good or bad, man is actually the arbiter of his own fate, and that it is his concept of himself that determines the world in which he lives. In other words, if you are experiencing ill health, knowing the truth about cause, you cannot attribute the illness to anything other than to the particular arrangement of the basic cause-substance, an arrangement which is defined by your concept 'I am unwell.' This is why you are told "Let the weak man say, 'I am strong'." (Joel 3:10), for by his assumption, the cause-substance – 'I AM' – is rearranged and must, therefore, manifest that which its rearrangement affirms. This principle governs every aspect of your life, be it social, financial, intellectual, or spiritual.

'I AM' is that reality to which, whatever happens, we must turn for an explanation of the phenomena of life. It is 'I AM's' concept of itself that determines the form and scenery of its existence. Everything depends upon its attitude towards itself; that which it will not affirm as true of itself cannot awaken in its world. That is, your concept of yourself, such as "I am strong," "I am secure," "I am loved," determines the world in which you live. In other words, when you say, "I am a man, I am a father, I am an American," you are not defining different 'I AMs;' you are defining different concepts or arrangements of the one cause-substance – the one 'I AM'. Even in the phenomena of nature, if the tree were articulate, it would say, "I am a tree, an apple tree, a fruitful tree".

When you know that consciousness is the one and only reality – conceiving itself to be something good, bad, or indifferent, and becoming that which it conceived itself to be – you are free from the tyranny of second causes, free from the belief that there are causes outside of your own mind that can affect your life.

In the state of consciousness of the individual is found the explanation of the phenomena of life. If man's concept of himself were different, everything in his world would be different. His concept of himself being what it is, everything in his world must be as it is.

Thus it is abundantly clear that there is only *one* I AM and *you* are that I AM. And while *I AM is infinite*, you, by your concept of yourself, are displaying only a limited aspect of the infinite 'I AM.'

*"Build thee more stately mansions, O my soul,*
*As the swift seasons roll!*
*Leave thy low-vaulted past!*
*Let each new temple, nobler than the last,*
*Shut thee from heaven with a dome more vast*
*Till thou at length art free,*
*Leaving thine outgrown shell by life's unresting sea!"*

# 2

# Consciousness

It is only by a change of consciousness, by actually changing your concept of yourself that you can "build more stately mansions" – the manifestations of higher and higher concepts. (By manifesting is meant experiencing the results of these concepts in your world.) It is of vital importance to understand clearly just what consciousness is.

The reason lies in the fact that *consciousness is the one and only reality, it is the first and only cause-substance of the phenomena of life*. Nothing has existence for man save through the consciousness he has of it. Therefore, it is to consciousness you must turn, for it is the only foundation on which the phenomena of life can be explained.

If we accept the idea of a first cause, it would follow that the evolution of that cause could never result in anything foreign to itself. That is, if the first cause-substance is light, all its evolutions, fruits and manifestations would remain light. The first cause-substance being consciousness, all its evolutions, fruits, and phenomena must remain consciousness. All that could be observed would be a higher or lower form or variation of the same thing. In other words, if your consciousness is the only reality, it must also be the *only* substance. Consequently, what appears to you as circumstances, conditions and even material objects are really only the products of your own consciousness. Nature, then, as a thing or a complex of things external to your mind, must be rejected. You and your environment cannot be regarded as existing separately. You and your world are *one*.

Therefore, you must turn from the objective appearance of things to the *subjective center* of things, your consciousness, if you truly desire to know the cause of the phenomena of life, and how to use this knowledge to realize your fondest dreams. In the midst of the apparent contradictions, antagonisms, and contrasts of your life, *there is only one principle at work,* only your consciousness operating. Difference does not consist in variety of substance, but in variety of arrangement of the same cause-substance, your consciousness.

The world moves with motiveless necessity. By this is meant that it has no motive of its own, but is under the necessity of manifesting your concept, the arrangement of your mind, and *your mind is always arranged in the image of all you believe and consent to as true.* The rich man, poor man, beggar man or thief are not different minds, but different arrangements of the same mind, in the same sense that a piece of steel, when magnetized, differs not in substance from its demagnetized state but in the arrangement and order of its molecules. A single electron revolving in a specified orbit constitutes the unit of magnetism. When a piece of steel or anything else is demagnetized, the revolving electrons have not stopped. Therefore, the magnetism has not gone out of existence. There is only a rearrangement of the particles, so that they produce no outside or perceptible effect. When particles are arranged at random, mixed up in all directions, the substance is said to be demagnetized; but when particles are marshalled in ranks so that a number of them face in one direction, the substance is a magnet. Magnetism is not generated; it is displayed. *Health, wealth, beauty, and genius are not created; they are only manifested* by the arrangement of your mind – that is, by your concept of yourself. The importance of this in your daily life should be immediately apparent.

The basic nature of the primal cause is consciousness. Therefore, the ultimate substance of all things is *consciousness.*

# 3

# *Power of Assumption*

Man's chief delusion is his conviction that there are *causes other than his own state of consciousness.* All that befalls a man – all that is done by him – all that comes from him – happens as a result of his state of consciousness. A man's consciousness is all that he thinks and desires and loves, all that he believes is true and consents to. That is why a change of consciousness is necessary before you can change your outer world. Rain falls as a result of a change in the temperature in the higher regions of the atmosphere, so, in like manner, a change of circumstance happens as a result of a change in your state of consciousness.

"Be ye transformed by the renewing of your mind."

To be transformed, the whole basis of your thoughts must change. But your thoughts cannot change unless you have *new ideas,* for you think from your ideas. All transformation begins with an intense, burning desire to be transformed. The first step in the 'renewing of the mind' is *desire.* You must want to be different before you can begin to change yourself. Then you must *make your future dream a present fact.* You do this by *assuming the feeling of your wish fulfilled.* By desiring to be other than what you are, you can create an ideal of the person you want to be and *assume that you are already that person.* If this assumption is persisted in until it becomes your dominant feeling, the attainment of your ideal is inevitable. The ideal you hope to achieve is always ready for an incarnation, but unless you yourself offer it human parentage, it is incapable of birth. Therefore, your attitude should be one in which – having desired to express a higher state – you alone accept the task of incarnating this new and greater value of yourself.

In giving birth to your ideal you must bear in mind that the methods of mental and spiritual knowledge are entirely different. This is a point that is truly understood by probably not more than one person in a million. You know a thing mentally by looking at it from the outside, by comparing it with other things, by analyzing it and defining it; whereas you can know a thing spiritually only by becoming it. You must be the thing itself and not merely talk about it or look at it. You must be like the moth in search of his idol, the flame,

> "who spurred with true desire, plunging at once into the sacred fire, folded his wings within, till he became one color and one substance with the flame. He only knew the flame who in it burned, and only he could tell who ne'er to tell returned."

Just as the moth in his desire to know the flame was willing to destroy himself, so must you in becoming a new person be willing to die to your present self.

You must be conscious of *being* healthy if you are to know what health is. You must be conscious of *being* secure if you are to know what security is. Therefore, to incarnate a new and greater value of yourself, you must assume that you already are what you want to be and then live by faith in this assumption – which is not yet incarnate in the body of your life – in confidence that this new value or state of consciousness will become incarnated through your absolute fidelity to the assumption that you are that which you desire to be. This is what wholeness means, what integrity means. They mean submission of the whole self to the feeling of the wish fulfilled in certainty that that new state of consciousness is the renewing of mind which transforms. There is no order in Nature corresponding to this willing submission of the self to the ideal beyond the self. Therefore, it is the height of folly to expect the incarnation of a new and greater concept of self to come about by natural evolutionary process. That which requires a state of consciousness to produce its effect obviously cannot be effected without such a state of consciousness, and in your ability to assume the feeling of a greater life, to assume a new concept of yourself, *you possess what the rest of Nature does not possess – Imagination – the instrument by which you create your world.*

Your imagination is the instrument, the means, whereby your redemption from slavery, sickness, and poverty is effected. If you refuse to assume the responsibility of the incarnation of a new and higher concept of yourself, then you *reject the means, the only means, whereby your redemption – that is, the attainment of your ideal – can be effected.*

Imagination is the only redemptive power in the universe. However, your nature is such that it is optional to you whether you remain in your present concept of yourself (a hungry being longing for freedom, health, and security) or choose to become the instrument of your own redemption, imagining yourself as that which you want to be, and thereby satisfying your hunger and redeeming yourself.

> "O be strong then, and brave, pure, patient and true;
> The work that is yours let no other hand do.
> For the strength for all need is faithfully given
> From the fountain within you – The Kingdom of Heaven."

# 4

# *Desire*

The changes which take place in your life *as a result of your changed concept of yourself* always appear to the unenlightened to be the result, not of a change of your consciousness, but of chance, outer cause, or coincidence. However, the only fate governing your life is the fate determined by your own concepts, your own assumptions; for an assumption, *though false*, if persisted in, will harden into fact. The ideal you seek and hope to attain will not manifest itself, will not be realized by you, until you have imagined that you are already that ideal. There is no escape for you except by a radical psychological transformation of yourself, except by your assumption of the feeling of your wish fulfilled. Therefore, make results or accomplishments the crucial test of your ability to use your imagination.

Everything depends on your attitude towards yourself. *That which you will not affirm as true of yourself can never be realized by you,* for that attitude alone is the necessary condition by which you realize your goal.

All transformation is based upon suggestion, and this can work only where you lay yourself completely open to an influence. You must abandon yourself to your ideal as a woman abandons herself to love, for complete abandonment of self to it is the way to union with your ideal. You must assume the feeling of the wish fulfilled until your assumption has all the sensory vividness of reality. *You must imagine that you are already experiencing what you desire.* That is, you must assume the feeling of the fulfillment of your desire until you are possessed by it and this feeling crowds all other ideas out of your consciousness.

The man who is not prepared for the conscious plunge into the assumption of the wish fulfilled in the faith that it is the only way to the realization of his dream is not yet ready to live *consciously* by the law of assumption, although there is no doubt that he does live by the law of assumption unconsciously. But for you who accept this principle and are ready to live by consciously assuming that your wish is already fulfilled, the adventure of life begins. To reach a higher level of being, you must assume a higher concept of yourself.

If you will not imagine yourself as other than what you are, then you remain as you are,

> "for if ye believe not that I am
> He, ye shall die in your sins."

If you do not believe that you are He (the person you want to be), then you remain as you are. Through the faithful systematic cultivation of the feeling of the wish fulfilled, *desire becomes the promise of its own fulfillment.* The assumption of the feeling of the wish fulfilled makes the future dream a present fact.

## 5

# *The Truth that Sets You Free*

The drama of life is a psychological one in which all the conditions, circumstances, and events of your life are brought to pass by your assumptions.

Since your life is determined by your assumptions, you are forced to recognize the fact that you are either a slave to your assumptions or their master. To become the master of your assumptions is the key to undreamed of freedom and happiness. You can attain this mastery by deliberate conscious control of your imagination. You determine your assumptions in this way: Form a mental image, a picture of the state desired, of the person you want to be. Concentrate your attention upon the feeling that you are already that person. First, visualize the picture in your consciousness. Then *feel* yourself to be in that state as though it actually formed your surrounding world. By your imagination that which was a mere mental image is changed into a seemingly solid reality.

The great secret is a controlled imagination and a well-sustained attention firmly and repeatedly focused on the object to be accomplished. It cannot be emphasized too much that, by creating an ideal within your mental sphere, by assuming that you are already that ideal, *you identify yourself with it and thereby transform yourself into its image.* This was called by the ancient teachers "Subjection to the will of God" or "Resting in the Lord", and the only true test of "Resting in the Lord" is that all who *do* rest are inevitably transformed into the image of that in which they rest. You become according to your resigned will, and your resigned will is your concept of yourself and all that you consent to and accept as true. You, assuming the feeling of your wish fulfilled and continuing therein, take upon yourself the results of that state; not assuming the feeling of your wish fulfilled, you are ever free of the results.

When you understand the redemptive function of imagination, *you hold in your hands the key to the solution of all your problems.* Every phase of your life is made by the exercise of your imagination. Determined imagination alone is the means of your progress, of the fulfilling of your dreams. *It is the beginning and end of all creating. The great secret is a controlled imagination and a well sustained attention firmly and repeatedly focused on the feeling of the wish fulfilled until it fills the mind and crowds all other ideas out of consciousness.* What greater gifts could be given you than to be told the Truth that will set you free? *The Truth that sets you free is that you can experience in imagination what you desire to experience in reality, and by maintaining this experience in imagination your desire will become an actuality.*

You are limited only by your uncontrolled imagination and lack of attention to the feeling of your wish fulfilled. When the imagination is not controlled and the attention not steadied on the feeling of the wish fulfilled, then no amount of prayer or piety or invocation will produce the desired effect. When you can call up at will whatsoever image you please, when the forms of your imagination are as vivid to you as the forms of nature, you are master of your fate.

*Visions of beauty and splendor,*
*Forms of a long-lost race,*
*Sounds and faces and voices,*
*From the fourth dimension of space –*

*And on through the universe boundless,*
*Our thoughts go lightning shod –*
*Some call it imagination,*
*And others call it God.*

# 6

# *Attention*

"A doubleminded man is unstable in all his ways."

JAMES 1:8

Attention is forceful in proportion to the narrowness of its focus, that is, when it is obsessed with a single idea or sensation. It is steadied and powerfully focused only by such an adjustment of the mind as permits you to see one thing only, for you steady the attention and increase its power by confining it. *The desire which realizes itself is always a desire upon which attention is exclusively concentrated,* for an idea is endowed with power only in proportion, to the degree of attention fixed on it. Concentrated observation is the attentive attitude directed toward some specific end. The attentive attitude involves selection, for when you pay attention, it signifies that you have decided to focus your attention on one object or state rather than on another.

Therefore, when you know what you want, you must deliberately focus your attention on the feeling of your wish fulfilled until that feeling fills the mind and crowds all other ideas out of consciousness.

The power of attention is the measure of your inner force. Concentrated observation of one thing shuts out other things and causes them to disappear. *The great secret of success is to focus the attention on the feeling of the wish fulfilled without permitting any distraction.* All progress depends upon an increase of attention. The ideas which impel you to action are those which dominate the consciousness, those which possess the attention.

> "This one thing I do, forgetting those things that are behind,
> I press toward the mark."

This means you, this one thing you can do, "forgetting those things that are behind." You can press toward the mark of filling your mind with the feeling of the wish fulfilled.

To the unenlightened man this will seem to be all fantasy, yet *all progress comes from those who do not take the accepted view, nor accept the world as it is.* As was stated heretofore, if you can imagine what you please, and if the forms of your thought are as vivid as the forms of nature, you are by virtue of the power of your imagination master of your fate.

*Your imagination is you yourself and the world as your imagination sees it is the real world.*

When you set out to master the movements of attention, which must be done if you would successfully alter the course of observed events, it is then you realize how little control you exercise over your imagination and how much it is dominated by sensory impressions and by a drifting on the tides of idle moods.

To aid in mastering the control of your attention practice this exercise. Night after night, just before you drift off to sleep, strive to hold your attention on the activities of the day *in reverse order.* Focus your attention on the last thing you did, that is, getting *in* to bed, and then move it backward in time over the events until you reach the first event of the day, getting *out* of bed. This is no easy exercise, but just as specific exercises greatly help in developing specific muscles, this will greatly help in developing the "muscle" of your attention. Your attention must be developed, controlled, and concentrated in order to change your concept of yourself successfully and thereby change your future. Imagination is able to do anything *but only according to the internal direction of your attention.* If you persist night after night, sooner or later you will awaken in yourself a centre of power and become conscious of your greater self, the real you. Attention is developed by repeated exercise or habit. Through habit an action becomes easier, and so in course of time gives rise to a facility or faculty, which can then be put to higher uses.

When you attain control of the internal direction of your attention, you will no longer stand in shallow water but will launch out into the deep of life. You will walk in the assumption of the wish fulfilled as on a foundation more solid even than earth.

# 7

# *Attitude*

Experiments recently conducted by Merle Lawrence (Princeton) and Adelbert Ames (Dartmouth) in the latter's psychology laboratory at Hanover, N.H., prove that what you see when you look at something *depends not so much on what is there as on the assumption you make when you look.* Since what we believe to be the "real" physical world is actually only an "assumptive" world, it is not surprising that these experiments prove that what appears to be solid reality is actually the result of "expectations" or "assumptions". Your assumptions determine not only what you see but also what you do, for they govern all your conscious and subconscious movements towards the fulfillment of themselves. Over a century ago this truth was stated by Emerson as follows:

> "As the world was plastic and fluid in the hands of God, so it is ever to so much of his attributes as we bring to it. To ignorance and sin, it is flint. They adapt themselves to it as they may, but in proportion as a man has anything in him divine, the firmament flows before him and takes his signet and form."

Your assumption is the hand of God moulding the firmament into the image of that which you assume. The assumption of the wish fulfilled is the high tide which lifts you easily off the bar of the senses where you have so long lain stranded. It lifts the mind into prophecy in the full right sense of the word; and if you have that controlled imagination and absorbed attention which it is possible to attain, you may be sure that all your assumption implies will come to pass.

When William Blake wrote,

> "What seems to be, is, to those to whom it seems to be,"

he was only repeating the eternal truth,

> "there is nothing unclean of itself; but to him that esteemeth anything to be unclean, to him it is unclean."
>
> ROMANS 14:14

Because there is nothing unclean *of itself* (or clean of itself) you should assume the best and think only of that which is lovely and of good report. It is not superior insight but ignorance of this law of assumption if you read into the greatness of men some littleness with which you may be familiar – or into some situation or circumstance an unfavorable conviction. *Your particular relationship to another influences your assumption with respect to that other and makes you see in him that which you do see.* If you can *change* your opinion of another, then what you now believe of him cannot be absolutely true but is only *relatively* true. The following is an actual case history illustrating how the law of assumption works:

One day a costume designer described to me her difficulties in working with a prominent theatrical producer. She was convinced that he unjustly criticized and rejected her best work and that often he was deliberately rude and unfair to her. Upon hearing her story, I explained that if she found the other rude and unfair, it was a sure sign that she, herself, was wanting and that it was not the producer, but herself that was in need of a new attitude. I told her that the power of this law of assumption and its practical application could be discovered only through experience, and that only by assuming that the situation was *already* what she wanted it to be could she prove that she could bring about the change desired. Her employer was merely bearing witness, telling her by his behavior what her *concept* of him was. I suggested that it was quite probable that she was carrying on conversations with him *in her mind* which were filled with criticism and recriminations. There was no doubt but that she was mentally arguing with the producer, for others only echo that which we whisper to them in secret. I asked her if it was not true that she talked to him *mentally*, and, if so, what those conversations were like. She confessed that every morning on her way to the theatre she told him just what she thought of him in a way she would never have dared address him in person. The intensity and force of her mental arguments with him automatically established his behavior towards her. She began to realize that all of us carry on mental conversations, but, unfortunately, on most occasions these conversations are argumentative… that we have only to observe the passerby on the street to prove this assertion… that so many people are mentally engrossed in conversation and few appear to be happy about it, but the very intensity of their feeling must lead them quickly to the unpleasant incident they themselves have mentally created and therefore must now encounter. When she realized what she had been doing, she agreed to change her attitude and to live this law faithfully by assuming that her job was highly satisfactory and her relationship with the producer was a very happy one. To do this she agreed that before going to sleep at night, on her way to work, and at other intervals during the day she would *imagine* that he had congratulated her on her fine designs and that she, in turn, had thanked him for his praise and kindness. To her great delight she soon discovered for herself that her own attitude was the cause of all that befell her.

The behavior of her employer miraculously reversed itself. His attitude, echoing as it had always done, that which she had assumed, now reflected her *changed* concept of him.

What she did was by the power of her imagination. Her persistent assumption influenced his behavior and determined his attitude toward her.

> "With the passport of desire on the wings of a controlled imagination she traveled into the future of her own predetermined experience."

Thus we see it is not facts, but that which we create in our imagination, which shapes our lives, for most of the conflicts of the day are due to the want of a little imagination to cast the beam out of our own eye. It is the exact and literal minded who live in a fictitious world. As this designer, by her controlled imagination, started the subtle change in her employer's mind, so can we, by the control of our own imagination and wisely directed feeling, solve our problems.

By the intensity of her imagination and feeling the designer cast a kind of enchantment on her producer's mind and caused him to think that his generous praise originated with him. Often our most elaborate and original thoughts are determined by another.

> "We should never be certain that it was not some woman treading in the wine-press who began that subtle change in men's mind, or that the passion did not begin in the mind of some shepherd boy, lighting up his eyes for a moment before it ran upon its way."
>
> William Butler Yeats

# 8

# *Renunciation*

> "There is no coal of character so dead that it will not glow and flame if but slightly turned."
>
> "Resist not evil."
>
> "Whosoever shall smite thee on thy right cheek, turn to him the other also."
>
> **MATTHEW 5:39**

There is a great difference between *resisting evil and renouncing it.* When you resist evil, you give it your attention; you continue to make it real. When you renounce evil, you take your attention from it and give your attention to what you want. Now is the time to control your imagination and

> "Give beauty for ashes, joy for mourning, praise for the spirit of heaviness, that they might be called trees of righteousness, the planting of the Lord that He might be glorified."

You give beauty for ashes when you concentrate your attention on things as you would like them to be rather than on things as they are. You give joy for mourning when you maintain a joyous attitude regardless of unfavorable circumstances. You give praise for the spirit of heaviness when you maintain a confident attitude instead of succumbing to despondency. In this quotation the Bible uses the word tree as a synonym for man. You become a tree of righteousness when the above mental states are a permanent part of your consciousness. You are a planting of the Lord when all your thoughts are *true* thoughts. He is "I AM" as described in Chapter One. "I AM" is glorified when your highest concept of yourself is manifested.

When you have discovered your own controlled imagination to be your saviour, your attitude will be completely altered without any diminution of religious feeling, and you will say of your controlled imagination

> "Behold this vine. I found it a wild tree, whose wanton strength had swollen into irregular twigs. But I pruned the plant and it grew temperate in its vain expense of useless leaves, and knotted as you see into these clean full clusters to repay the hand that wisely wounded it."

By vine is meant your imagination, which in its uncontrolled state, expends its energy in useless or destructive thoughts and feelings. But you, just as the vine is pruned by cutting away its useless branches and roots, prune your imagination *by withdrawing your attention from all unlovely and destructive ideas and concentrating on the ideal you wish to attain.* The happier, more noble life you will experience will be the result of wisely pruning your own imagination. Yes, be pruned of all unlovely thoughts and feelings that you may

> "Think truly, and thy thoughts shall the world's famine feed;
> Speak truly, and each word of thine shall be a fruitful seed;
> Live truly, and thy life shall be a great and noble creed."

9

# *Preparing Your Place*

> "And all mine are thine, and thine are mine."
>
> JOHN 17:10

> "Thrust in thy sickle, and reap; for the time is come for thee to reap; for the harvest of the earth is ripe."
>
> REVELATION 14:15

All is yours. Do not go seeking for that which you are. Appropriate it, claim it, assume it. *Everything* depends upon your concept of yourself. That which you do not claim as true of yourself, cannot be realized by you. The promise is

> "Whosoever hath, to him it shall be given, and he shall have more abundance; but whosoever hath not, from him shall be taken away even that which he seemeth to have."

Hold fast, in your imagination, to all that is lovely and of good report, for the lovely and the good are essential in your life if it is to be worthwhile. Assume it. You do this by imagining that you *already are* what you want to be – and *already have* what you want to have.

> "As a man thinketh in his heart so is he."

Be still and know that you are that which you desire to be, and you will never have to search for it.

In spite of your appearance of freedom of action, you obey, as everything else does, the law of assumption. Whatever you may think of the question of free will, the truth is *your experiences throughout your life are determined by your assumptions* – whether conscious or unconscious. An assumption *builds a bridge of incidents that lead inevitably to the fulfillment of itself.*

Man believes the future to be the natural development of the past. But the law of assumption clearly shows that this is not the case. Your assumption places you psychologically where you are not *physically;* then your senses pull you back from where you were psychologically to where you are physically. *It is these psychological forward motions that produce your physical forward motions in time.* Pre-cognition permeates all the scriptures of the world.

> "In my Father's house are many mansions; If it were not so, I would have told you. I go to prepare a place for you. And if I go and prepare a place for you, I will come again and receive you unto myself: that where I am, there ye may be also… And now I have told you before it came to pass, that, when it is come to pass, ye might believe."

The "I" in this quotation is your imagination which goes into the future, into one of the many mansions. Mansion is the state desired… telling of an event before it occurs physically is simply feeling yourself into the state desired until it has the tone of reality. *You go and prepare a place for yourself by imagining yourself into the feeling of your wish fulfilled.* Then, you speed from this state of the wish fulfilled – where you have not been physically – back to where you were physically a moment ago. Then, with an irresistible forward movement, you move forward across a series of events to the physical realization of your wish, that where you have been in imagination, there you will be in the flesh also.

"Unto the place from whence the rivers come, thither they return again."

ECCLESIASTES 1:7

# 10

# *Creation*

> "I am God, declaring the end from the beginning, and from ancient times things that are not yet done."
>
> Isaiah 46:10

Creation is finished. Creativeness is only a deeper receptiveness, for the entire contents of all time and all space while experienced in a time sequence actually co-exist in an infinite and eternal now. In other words, all that you ever have been or ever will be – in fact, all that mankind ever was or ever will be – exists now. This is what is meant by creation, and the statement that creation is finished means nothing is ever to be created, it is only to be manifested. *What is called creativeness is only becoming aware of what already is.* You simply become aware of increasing portions of that which already exists. The fact that you can never be anything that you are not already or experience anything not already existing explains the experience of having an acute feeling of having heard before what is being said, or having met before the person being met for the first time, or having seen before a place or thing being seen for the first time.

*The whole of creation exists in you, and it is your destiny to become increasingly aware of its infinite wonders and to experience ever greater and grander portions of it.*

If creation is finished, and all events are taking place now, the question that springs naturally to the mind is "what determines your time track?" That is, what determines the events which you encounter? And the answer is *your concept of yourself.* Concepts determine the route that attention follows. Here is a good test to prove this fact. Assume the feeling of your wish fulfilled and observe the route that your attention follows. You will observe that as long as you remain faithful to your assumption, so long will your attention be confronted with images clearly related to that assumption. For example; if you assume that you have a wonderful business, you will notice how *in your imagination* your attention is focused on incident after incident relating to that assumption. Friends congratulate you, tell you how lucky you are. Others are envious and critical. From there your attention goes to larger offices, bigger bank balances, and many other similarly related events. Persistence in this assumption will result in *actually experiencing in fact that which you assumed.*

The same is true regarding any concept. If your concept of yourself is that you are a failure, you would encounter in your imagination a whole series of incidents in conformance to that concept.

Thus it is clearly seen how you, by your concept of yourself, determine your present, that is, the particular portion of creation which you now experience, and your future, that is, the particular portion of creation which you will experience.

# 11

# *Interference*

You are free to choose the concept you will accept of yourself. Therefore, you possess the power of *intervention*, the power which enables you to *alter the course of your future.* The process of rising from your present concept to a higher concept of yourself is the means of all true progress. The higher concept is waiting for you to incarnate it in the world of experience.

> "Now unto Him that is able to do exceeding abundantly above all that we ask or think, according to the power that worketh in us. Unto him be glory."
>
> **EPHESIANS 3:20**

Him, that is able to do more than you can ask or think, *is your imagination*, and the *power that worketh in us* is *your attention.* Understanding imagination to be HIM that is able to do all that you ask, and attention to be the power by which you create your world, you can now build your ideal world. Imagine yourself to be the ideal you dream of and desire. Remain attentive to this imagined state and as fast as you completely feel that you are already this ideal it will manifest itself as *reality* in your world.

> "He was in the world, and the world was made by Him and the world knew him not."

"The mystery hid from the ages; Christ in you, the hope of glory."

The "He," in the first of these quotations is your imagination. As previously explained, there is only one substance. This substance is consciousness. It is your imagination which forms this substance into concepts, which concepts are then manifested as conditions, circumstances, and physical objects. *Thus imagination made your world.* This supreme truth, with but few exceptions, man is not conscious of.

The mystery, *Christ in you,* referred to in the second quotation, is your imagination, by which your world is molded. The hope of glory is your awareness of the ability to rise perpetually to higher levels.

Christ is not to be found in history nor in external forms. You find Christ only when you become aware of the fact that *your imagination* is the only redemptive power. When this is discovered, the "towers of dogma will have heard the trumpets of Truth, and, like the walls of Jericho, crumble to dust."

12

# *Subjective Control*

Your imagination is able to do all that you ask *in proportion to the degree of your attention.* All progress, all fulfillment of desire, depend upon the control and concentration of your attention. Attention may be either attracted from without or directed from within. Attention is attracted from without when you are consciously occupied with the external impressions of the immediate present. The very lines of this page are attracting your attention from without. Your attention is directed from within when you deliberately choose what you will be preoccupied with mentally. It is obvious that in the objective world your attention is not only attracted by but is constantly directed to external impressions. But, your control in the *subjective state* is almost non-existent, for in this state attention is usually the servant and not the master – the passenger and not the navigator – of your world. There is an enormous difference between attention directed objectively and attention directed subjectively, and the *capacity to change your future depends on the latter.* When you are able to control the movements of your attention in the subjective world, you can modify or alter your life as you please. But this control cannot be achieved if you allow your attention to be attracted constantly from without. Each day, set yourself the task of deliberately withdrawing your attention from the objective world and of focusing it *subjectively.* In other words, concentrate on those thoughts or moods which you deliberately determine. Then those things that now restrict you will fade and drop away. The day you achieve control of the movements of your attention in the subjective world, you are master of your fate.

You will no longer accept the dominance of outside conditions or circumstances. You will not accept life on the basis of the world without. Having achieved control of the movements of your attention, and having discovered the mystery hid from the ages, that *Christ in you is your imagination,* you will assert the supremacy of *imagination* and put all things in subjection to it.

# 13

# *Acceptance*

> "Man's Perceptions are not bounded by organs of Perception: he perceives more than sense (though ever so acute) can discover."

However much you seem to be living in a material world, *you are actually living in a world of imagination.* The outer, physical events of life are the fruit of forgotten blossom-times – results of previous and usually forgotten states of consciousness. They are the ends running true to oft-times forgotten imaginative origins.

Whenever you become completely absorbed in an emotional state, you are at that moment assuming the feeling of the state fulfilled. If persisted in, whatsoever you are intensely emotional about you will experience in your world. These periods of absorption, of concentrated attention, are the beginnings of the things you harvest. It is in such moments that you are exercising your creative power – the only creative power there is. At the end of these periods, or moments of absorption, you speed from these imaginative states (where you have *not been* physically) to where you were physically an instant ago. In these periods, the imagined state is so real that when you return to the objective world and find that it is not the same as the imagined state, it is an actual shock. You have seen something in imagination with such vividness that you now wonder whether the evidence of your senses can now be believed, and like Keats, you ask,

> "was it a vision or a waking dream? Fled is that music...
> Do I wake or sleep?"

This shock reverses your time sense. By this is meant that *instead of your experience resulting from your past, it now becomes the result of being in imagination where you have not yet been physically.* In effect, this moves you across a bridge of incident to the physical realization of your imagined state. The man who at will can assume whatever state he pleases has found the keys to the Kingdom of Heaven. The keys are *desire, imagination, and a steadily focused attention on the feeling of the wish fulfilled.* To such a man any undesirable objective fact is no longer a reality and the ardent wish no longer a dream.

> "Prove me now herewith, saith the Lord of hosts, if I will not open you the windows of heaven, and pour you out a blessing, that there shall not be room enough to receive it."
>
> MALACHI 3:10

The windows of heaven may not be opened and the treasures seized by a strong will, but they open of themselves and present their treasures as a free gift – a gift that comes when absorption reaches such a degree that it results in a feeling of complete acceptance. The passage from your present state to the feeling of your wish fulfilled is not across a gap. There is continuity between the so-called real and unreal. To cross from one state to the other, you simply extend your feelers, trust your touch and enter fully into the spirit of what you are doing.

> "Not by might nor by power but by my spirit, saith the Lord of hosts."

Assume the spirit, the feeling of the wish fulfilled, and you will have opened the windows to receive the blessing. To assume a state is to get into the spirit of it. Your triumphs will be a surprise only to those who did not know your hidden passage from the state of longing to the assumption of the wish fulfilled.

The Lord of hosts will not respond to your wish until you have assumed the feeling of already being what you want to be, for *acceptance is the channel of His action.* Acceptance is the Lord of hosts in action.

# 14

# *The Effortless Way*

The principle of "Least Action" governs everything in physics from the path of a planet to the path of a pulse of light. Least Action is the minimum of energy, multiplied by the minimum of time. Therefore, in moving from your present state to the state desired, you must use the minimum of energy and take the shortest possible time. Your journey from one state of consciousness to another is a psychological one, so, to make the journey, you must employ the psychological equivalent of 'Least Action,' and the psychological equivalent is mere assumption.

The day you fully realize the power of assumption, you discover that it works in complete conformity with this principle. It works by means of attention, minus effort. Thus, with least action through an assumption you hurry without haste and reach your goal without effort.

Because creation is finished, *what you desire already exists.* It is excluded from view because you can see only the contents of your own consciousness. It is the function of an assumption to call back the excluded view and restore full vision. *It is not the world but your assumptions that change.* An assumption brings the invisible into sight. It is nothing more nor less than seeing with the eye of God, i.e., imagination.

> "For the Lord seeth not as a man seeth, for man looketh on the outward appearance, but the Lord looketh on the heart."

The heart is the primary organ of sense, hence the first cause of experience. When you look "on the heart", you are looking at your assumptions: assumptions determine your experience. Watch your assumption with all diligence for out of it are the issues of life. Assumptions have the power of objective realization. Every event in the visible world is the result of an assumption or idea in the unseen world.

The present moment is all-important, for it is only in the present moment that our assumptions can be controlled. The future must become the present in your mind if you would wisely operate the law of assumption. The future becomes the present when you imagine that you already are what you will be when your assumption is fulfilled. Be still (least action) and know that you are that which you desire to be. The end of longing should be Being. Translate your dream into Being. Perpetual construction of future states without the consciousness of already being them, that is, picturing your desire without actually assuming the feeling of the wish fulfilled, is the fallacy and mirage of mankind.

It is simply futile day-dreaming.

# 15

# *The Crown of the Mysteries*

The assumption of the wish fulfilled is the ship that carries you over the unknown seas to the fulfillment of your dream. *The assumption is everything; realization is subconscious and effortless.*

"Assume a virtue if you have it not."

Act on the assumption that you already possess that which you sought.

> "Blessed is she that believed; for there shall be a performance
> of those things which were told her from the Lord."

As the Immaculate Conception is the foundation of the Christian mysteries, so the Assumption is their crown. Psychologically, the Immaculate Conception means the *birth of an idea* in your own consciousness unaided by another. For instance, when you have a specific wish or hunger or longing it is an immaculate conception in the sense that no physical person or thing plants it in your mind. It is self-conceived. Every man is the Mary of the Immaculate Conception and birth to his idea must give. The Assumption is the crown of the mysteries because it is the highest use of consciousness. When in imagination you assume the feeling of the wish fulfilled, *you are mentally lifted up to a higher level.* When, through your persistence, this assumption becomes actual fact, you automatically find yourself on a higher level (that is, you have achieved your desire) in your objective world. Your assumption guides all your conscious and subconscious movements towards its suggested end so inevitably that it *actually dictates the events.*

The drama of life is a psychological one and the whole of it is written and produced by *your assumptions.*

Learn the art of assumption, for only in this way can you create your own happiness.

# 16

# *Personal Impotence*

Self-surrender is essential, and by that is meant the confession of personal impotence.

"I can of mine own self do nothing."

Since creation is finished it is impossible to *force* anything into being. The example of magnetism previously given is a good illustration. You cannot make magnetism; it can only be displayed. You cannot make the *law* of magnetism. If you want to build a magnet, you can do so only by conforming to the law of magnetism. In other words, you surrender yourself or yield to the law. In like manner, when you use the faculty of assumption, you are *conforming* to a law just as real as the law governing magnetism. *You can neither create nor change the law of assumption.* It is in this respect that you are impotent. You can only yield or conform, and since all of your experiences are the result of your assumptions, (consciously or unconsciously), the value of consciously using the power of assumption surely must be obvious.

Willingly identify yourself with that which you most desire, knowing that it will find expression through you. Yield to the feeling of the wish fulfilled and be consumed as its victim, then rise as the prophet of *the law of assumption.*

# 17

# *All Things are Possible*

It is of great significance that the truth of the principles outlined in this book have been proven time and again by the personal experiences of the Author. Throughout the past twenty-five years, he has applied these principles and proved them successful in innumerable instances. He attributes to an unwavering assumption of his wish already being fulfilled every success that he has achieved. He was confident that by these fixed assumptions his desires were predestined to be fulfilled. Time and again he assumed the feeling of his wish fulfilled and continued in his assumption until that which he desired was completely realized.

Live your life in a sublime spirit of confidence and determination; disregard appearances, conditions, in fact all evidence of your senses that deny the fulfillment of your desire. Rest in the assumption that you are already what you want to be, for in that determined assumption you and your Infinite Being are merged in creative unity, *and with your Infinite Being (God) all things are possible.* God never fails.

> "For who can stay His hand or say unto Him, 'What doest thou'?"

Through the mastery of your assumptions you are in very truth enabled to *master life*. It is thus that the ladder of life is ascended: thus the ideal is realized. The clue to the real purpose of life is to surrender yourself to your ideal with such awareness of its *reality* that you begin to live the life of the ideal and no longer your own life as it was prior to this surrender.

> "He calleth things that are not seen as though they were, and the unseen becomes seen."

Each assumption has its corresponding world. If you are truly observant, you will notice the power of your assumptions to change circumstances which appear wholly immutable.

You, by your conscious assumptions, determine the nature of the world in which you live. Ignore the present state and assume the wish fulfilled. Claim it; *it will respond.* The law of assumption is the means by which the fulfillment of your desires may be realized. Every moment of your life, *consciously or unconsciously*, you are assuming a feeling. You can no more avoid assuming a feeling than you can avoid eating and drinking. All you can do is control the nature of your assumptions.

Thus it is clearly seen that the control of your assumption is the key you now hold to an ever expanding, happier, more noble life.

# 18

# *Be Ye Doers*

"Be ye doers of the word and not hearers only, deceiving your own selves. For if any be a hearer of the word, and not a doer, he is like unto a man beholding his natural face in a glass and goeth his way, and straightway forgetteth what manner of man he was. But whoso looketh into the perfect law of liberty, and continue therein, he being not a forgetful hearer but a doer of the work, this man shall be blessed in his deed."

**James 1:22-25**

The word in this quotation means idea, concept, or desire. You deceive yourself by "hearing only" when you expect your desire to be fulfilled through mere wishful thinking. Your desire is what you want to be, and looking at yourself "in a glass" *is seeing yourself in imagination as that person.* Forgetting "what manner of man" you are is *failing to persist in your assumption.* The "perfect law of liberty" is the law which makes possible liberation from limitation, that is, the law of assumption. To continue in the perfect law of liberty is to persist in the assumption that your desire is already fulfilled. You are not a "forgetful hearer" when you keep the feeling of your wish fulfilled constantly alive in your consciousness. This makes you a "doer of the work," and you are blessed in your deed by the inevitable realization of your desire.

You must be *doers* of the law of assumption, for without application, the most profound understanding will not produce any desired result.

Frequent reiteration and repetition of important basic truths runs through these pages. Where the law of assumption is concerned – the law that sets man free – this is a good thing. It should be made clear again and again even at the risk of repetition. The real truth-seeker will welcome this aid in concentrating his attention upon the *law which sets him free.*

The parable of the Master's condemnation of the servant who neglected to use the talent given him is clear and unmistakable. Having discovered within yourself the key to the Treasure House, you should be like the good servant who, by wise use, multiplied by many times the talents entrusted to him. *The talent entrusted to you is the power to consciously determine your assumption.* The talent not used, like the limb not exercised, withers and finally atrophies.

What you must strive after is *being.* In order to do, it is necessary to be. *The end of yearning is to be.* Your concept of yourself can only be driven out of consciousness by *another* concept of yourself. By creating an ideal in your mind, you can identify yourself with it until you become one and the same with the ideal, thereby transforming yourself into it.

The dynamic prevails over the static; the active over the passive. One who is a doer is magnetic and therefore infinitely more creative than any who merely hear. Be among the doers.

# 19

# *Essentials*

The essential points in the successful use of the law of assumption are these: First, and above all, *yearning, longing; intense, burning desire.* With all your heart you must want to be different from what you are. Intense, burning desire *is* the mainspring of action, the beginning of all successful ventures. In every great passion desire is concentrated.

> "As the hart panteth after the water brooks, so panteth my soul after Thee, O God."
>
> "Blessed are they that hunger and thirst after righteousness for they shall be filled."

Here the soul is interpreted as the sum total of all you believe, think, feel, and accept as true; in other words, your present level of awareness, God means I AM, the source and fulfillment of all desires. This quotation describes how your present level of awareness longs to transcend itself. *Righteousness is the consciousness of already being what you want to be.*

Second, *cultivate physical immobility,* a physical incapability not unlike the state described by Keats in his 'Ode to a Nightingale'.

> "A drowsy numbness pains my senses, as though of hemlock
> I had drunk."

It is a state akin to sleep, but one in which you are still in control of the direction of attention. You must learn to induce this state at will, but experience has taught that it is more easily induced after a substantial meal, or when you wake in the morning feeling very loath to arise. Then you are naturally disposed to enter this state. The value of physical immobility shows itself in the accumulation of mental force which absolute stillness brings with it. It increases your power of concentration.

"Be still and know that I am God."

In fact, the greater energies of the mind seldom break forth save when the body is stilled and the door of the senses closed to the objective world.

The third and last thing to do is to *experience in your imagination what you would experience in reality had you achieved your goal.* Imagine that you possess a quality or something you desire which hitherto has not been yours. Surrender yourself completely to this feeling until your whole being is possessed by it. This state differs from reverie in this respect: it is the result of a *controlled imagination and a steadied, concentrated attention,* whereas reverie is the result of an uncontrolled imagination – usually just a day dream. In the controlled state, a minimum of effort suffices to keep your consciousness filled with the feeling of the wish fulfilled. The physical and mental immobility of this state is a powerful aid to voluntary attention and a major factor of minimum effort.

The application of these three points:

1. Desire
2. Physical immobility
3. The assumption of the wish already fulfilled

is the way to at-one-ment or *union with your objective.*

One of the most prevalent misunderstandings is that this law works only for those having a devout or a religious objective. This is a fallacy.

It works just as impersonally as the law of electricity works. It can be used for greedy, selfish purposes as well as noble ones. But it should always be borne in mind that ignoble thoughts and actions inevitably result in unhappy consequences.

# 20

# *Righteousness*

In the preceding chapter righteousness was defined as the *consciousness of already being what you want to be.* This is the true psychological meaning and obviously does not refer to adherence to moral codes, civil law or religious precepts. You cannot attach too much importance to being righteous. In fact, the entire Bible is permeated with admonition and exhortations on this subject.

> "Break off thy sins by righteousness."
>
> **Daniel 4:27**

> "My righteousness I hold fast, and will not let it go: my heart shall not reproach me so long as I live."
>
> **Job 27:6**

> "My righteousness shall answer for me in time to come."
>
> **Genesis 30:33**

Very often the words "sin" and "righteousness" are used in the same quotation. This is a logical contrast of opposites and becomes enormously significant in the light of the psychological meaning of righteousness and the psychological meaning of sin. Sin means *to miss the mark.* Not to attain your desire, not to be the person you want to be is sinning. Righteousness is the consciousness of already being what you want to be. It is a changeless educative law that effects must follow causes. Only by righteousness can you be saved from sinning.

There is a widespread misunderstanding as to what it means to be "saved from sin." The following example will suffice to demonstrate this misunderstanding and to establish the truth. A person living in abject poverty may believe that by means of some religious or philosophical activity he can be "saved from sin" and his life improved as a result. If, however, he continues to live in the same state of poverty it is obvious that what he believed was not the truth, and, in fact, he was not "saved". On the other hand, he can be saved by *righteousness*. The successful use of the law of assumption would have the inevitable result of an actual change in his life. He would no longer live in poverty. He would no longer miss the mark. He would be *saved from sin.*

> "Except your righteousness shall exceed the righteousness of the scribes and Pharisees, ye shall in no wise enter into the kingdom of Heaven."
>
> **MATTHEW 5:20**

Scribes and Pharisees means those who are influenced and governed by the outer appearances – the rules and customs of the society in which they live, the vain desire to be thought well of by other men. Unless this state of mind is exceeded, your life will be one of limitation – of failure to attain your desires – of missing the mark – of sin. This righteousness is exceeded by *true righteousness,* which is always the consciousness of *already being* that which you want to be.

One of the greatest pitfalls in attempting to use the law of assumption is focusing your attention on *things*, on a new home, a better job, a bigger bank balance. This is not the righteousness without which you "die in your sins." Righteousness is not the thing *itself; it is the consciousness, the feeling of already being the person you want to be, of already having the thing you desire.*

> "Seek ye first the kingdom of God, and His righteousness; and all these things shall be added unto you."
>
> MATTHEW 6:33

The kingdom (entire creation) of God (your I AM) is within you. Righteousness is the awareness that you *already* possess it all.

# 21

# *Free Will*

The question is often asked, "What should be done between the assumption of the wish fulfilled and its realization?" *Nothing.* It is a delusion that, other than assuming the feeling of the wish fulfilled you can do anything to aid the realization of your desire. You think that you can do something, you want to do something; but, actually you can do nothing *The illusion of the free will to do is but ignorance of the law of assumption* upon which all action is based. Everything happens automatically. All that befalls you, all that is done by you – *happens.* Your assumptions, *conscious or unconscious,* direct all thought and action to their fulfillment. To understand the law of assumption, to be convinced of its truth, means getting rid of all the illusions about free will to act. Free will actually means *freedom to select any idea you desire.* By assuming the idea *already* to be a fact, it is converted into reality. Beyond that, *free will ends,* and everything happens in harmony with the concept assumed.

> "I can of mine ownself do nothing ... because I seek not mine own will, but the will of the Father which hath sent Me."

In this quotation the Father obviously refers to God. In an earlier chapter, God is defined as I AM. Since creation is finished, the Father is never in a position of saying *"I will be."* In other words, everything exists and the infinite I AM consciousness can speak only in the *present tense.*

"Not my will but thine be done."

"I will be" is a confession that *"I am not"*. The Father's Will is *always* "I AM". Until you realize that YOU are the Father (there is only one I AM and your infinite self is that I AM), your will is always *"I will be."*

In the law of assumption your *consciousness of being* is the Father's will. The mere wish without this consciousness is the "my will". This great quotation, so little understood, is a perfect statement of the law of assumption.

It is impossible to *do* anything. You must *be* in order to do.

If you had a different concept of yourself, everything would be different. You are *what you are,* so everything *is as it is*. The events which you observe are determined by the concept you have of yourself. If you change your concept of yourself, the events ahead of you in time are altered, but, thus altered, they *form again a deterministic sequence* starting from the moment of this changed concept. You are a being with powers of intervention, which enable you, by a change of consciousness, to alter the course of observed events – in fact, to *change your future.*

Deny the evidence of the senses, and assume the feeling of the wish fulfilled. Inasmuch as your assumption is *creative* and forms an atmosphere, your assumption, if it be a noble one, increases your assurance and helps you to reach a higher level of being. If, on the other hand, your assumption be an unlovely one, it hinders you and makes your downward way swifter. Just as the lovely assumptions create a harmonious atmosphere, so the hard and bitter feelings create a hard and bitter atmosphere.

> "Whatsoever things are pure, just, lovely, of good report, think on these things."

This means to make your assumptions the highest, noblest, happiest concepts. There is no better time to start than *now.* The present moment is always the most opportune in which to eliminate all unlovely assumptions and to concentrate only on the good. As well as yourself, claim for others their Divine inheritance. See only their good and the good in them. Stir the highest in others to confidence and self-assertion, by your sincere assumption of their good and you will be their prophet and their healer, for an inevitable fulfillment awaits all sustained assumptions.

*You win by assumption what you can never win by force.* An assumption is a certain motion of consciousness. This motion, like all motion, exercises an influence on the surrounding substance, causing it to take the shape of, echo, and reflect the assumption. A change of fortune is a new direction and outlook, merely a change in arrangement of the same mind substance – *consciousness.*

If you would change your life, you must begin at the very source *with your own basic concept of self.* Outer change, becoming part of organizations, political bodies, religious bodies, is not enough. The cause goes deeper. The essential change must take place *in yourself,* in your own concept of self. You must assume that you *are* what you want to be and continue therein, for the *reality of your assumption has its being in complete independence of objective fact,* and will clothe itself in flesh if you persist in the feeling of the wish fulfilled. When you know that assumptions, if persisted in, harden into facts, then events which seem to the uninitiated mere accidents will be understood by you to be the logical and inevitable *effects* of your assumption.

The important thing to bear in mind is that you have *infinite free will in choosing your assumptions,* but no power to determine conditions and events. *You can create nothing, but your assumption determines what portion of creation you will experience.*

# 22

# *Persistence*

"And He said unto them, Which of you shall have a friend, and shall go unto him at midnight, and say unto him, Friend, lend me three loaves; for a friend of mine in his journey is come to me, and I have nothing to set before him? and he from within shall answer and say. Trouble me not; the door is now shut, and my children are with me in bed; I cannot rise and give thee. I say unto you. Though he will not rise and give him, because he is his friend, yet because of his importunity he will rise and give him as many as he needeth. And I say unto you. Ask, and it shall be given you; seek, and ye shall find; knock, and it shall be opened unto you."

LUKE 11:5-9

There are three principal characters in this quotation; you and the two friends mentioned. The first friend is a *desired state of consciousness.* The second friend is a *desire seeking fulfillment.* Three is the symbol of wholeness, completion. Loaves symbolize substance. The shut door symbolizes the senses which separate the seen from the unseen. Children in bed means ideas that are dormant. Inability to rise means a desired state of consciousness cannot rise to you, you must rise to it. Importunity means demanding persistency, a kind of brazen impudence. *Ask, seek* and *knock* mean *assuming the consciousness of already having what you desire.*

Thus the scriptures tell you that you must persist in rising to (assuming) the consciousness of your wish already being fulfilled. The promise is definite that if you are shameless in your impudence in assuming that you *already have* that which your senses deny, it shall be given unto you – *your desire shall be attained.*

The Bible teaches the necessity of persistence by the use of many stories. When Jacob sought a blessing from the Angel with whom he wrestled, he said

> "I will not let thee go, except thou bless me."

When the Shunammite sought the help of Elisha, she said,

> "As the Lord liveth, and as thy soul liveth, I will not leave thee, and he arose and followed her."

The same idea is expressed in another passage:

> "And he spake a parable unto them that men ought always to pray, and not to faint; saying, There was in a city a Judge, which feared not God, neither regarded man, and there was a widow in that city; and she came unto him, saying, Avenge me of mine adversary. And he would not for a while; but afterward he said within himself, Though I fear not God, nor regard man; yet because this widow troubleth me, I will avenge her, lest she weary me by her continual coming."
>
> **Luke 18:1-5**

The basic truth underlying each of these stories is that desire springs from the awareness of ultimate attainment and that persistence in maintaining the consciousness of the desire already being fulfilled results in its fulfillment.

It is not enough to feel yourself into the state of the answered prayer; you must persist in that state. That is the reason for the injunction

> 'man ought always to pray and not to faint';

here, to *pray means to give thanks for already having what you desire.* Only persistency in the assumption of the wish fulfilled can cause those subtle changes in your mind which result in the desired change in your life. It matters not whether they be "Angels," "Elisha," or "reluctant judges"; all *must* respond in harmony with your persistent assumption. When it appears that people other than yourself in your world do not act toward you as you would like, it is not due to reluctance on their part but a lack of *persistence* in your assumption of your life already being as you want it to be. Your assumption, to be effective cannot be a single isolated act; it must be a maintained attitude of the wish fulfilled.

# 23

# *Case Histories*

It will be extremely helpful at this point to cite a number of specific examples of the successful application of this law. *Actual case histories are given.* In each of these, the problem is clearly defined and the way imagination was used to attain the required state of consciousness is fully described. In each of these instances, the author of this book was either personally concerned or was told the facts by the person involved.

**1**

This is a story with every detail of which I am personally familiar.

In the spring of 1943 a recently drafted soldier was stationed in a large army camp in Louisiana. He was intensely eager to get out of the army but only in an entirely honorable way.

The only way he could do this was to apply for a discharge. The application then required the approval of his commanding officer to become effective. Based on army regulations, the decision of the commanding officer was final and could not be appealed. The soldier, following all the necessary procedure applied for a discharge. Within four hours this application was returned – marked "disapproved." Convinced he could not appeal the decision to any higher authority, military or civilian, he turned within to his own consciousness, determined to rely on the law of assumption.

The soldier realized that his consciousness was the only reality, that his particular state of consciousness determined the events he would en-counter.

That night, in the interval between getting into bed and falling asleep, he concentrated on consciously using the law of assumption. *In imagination* he felt himself to be in his own apartment in New York City. He visualized his apartment, that is, in his mind's eye he actually saw his own apartment, mentally picturing each one of the familiar rooms with all the furnishings vividly real.

With this picture clearly visualized, and lying flat on his back, he completely relaxed physically. In this way he induced a state bordering on sleep, at the same time retaining control of the direction of his attention. When his body was completely immobilized, he *assumed* that he was in his own room and felt himself to be lying in his own bed – a very different feeling from that of lying on an army cot. In imagination, he rose from the bed, walked from room to room touching various pieces of furniture. He then went to the window and, with his hands resting on the sill looked out on the street on which his apartment faced. *So vivid was all this in his imagination* that he saw in detail the pavement, the railings, the trees and the familiar red brick of the building on the opposite side of the street. He then returned to his bed and felt himself drifting off to sleep. He knew that it was most important in the successful use of this law that at the actual point of falling asleep his consciousness be filled with the assumption that he was already what he wanted to be. All that he did in imagination was based on the assumption that he was no longer in the army. Night after night the soldier enacted this drama. Night after night in imagination he felt himself, honorably discharged, back in his home seeing all the familiar surroundings and falling asleep in his own bed. This continued for eight nights. For eight days, his objective experience continued to be directly opposite to his subjective experience in consciousness each night, before going to sleep. On the ninth day orders came through from Battalion headquarters for the soldier to fill out a new application for his discharge. Shortly after this was done he was ordered to report to the Colonel's office. During the discussion the Colonel asked him if he was still desirous of getting out of the army. Upon receiving an affirmative reply, the Colonel said that he personally disagreed, and while he had strong objections to approving of the discharge, he had decided to overlook these objections and to approve it. Within a few hours the application was approved and the soldier, now a civilian, was on a train bound for home.

## 2

This is a striking story of an extremely successful businessman demonstrating the power of imagination and the law of assumption. I know this family intimately and all the details were told to me by the son described herein.

The story begins when he was twenty years old. He was next to the oldest in a large family of nine brothers and one sister. The father was one of the partners in a small merchandising business. In his eighteenth year the brother referred to in this story left the country in which they lived and traveled two thousand miles to enter college and complete his education. Shortly after his first year in college, he was called home because of a tragic event in connection with his father's business. Through the machinations of his associates, the father was not only forced out of his business but was the object of false accusations impugning his character and integrity. At the same time he was deprived of his rightful share in the equity of the business. The result was he found himself largely discredited and almost penniless. It was under these circumstances that the son was called home from college.

He returned, his heart filled with one great resolution. He was determined that he would become outstandingly successful in business. The first thing he and his father did was to use the little money they had to start their own business. They rented a small store on a side street not far from the large business of which the father had been one of the principal owners. There they started a business bent upon real service to the community. It was shortly thereafter that the son, with instinctive awareness that it was bound to work, deliberately used imagination to attain an almost fantastic objective.

Every day on the way to and from work he passed the building of his father's former business – the biggest business of its kind in the country. It was one of the largest buildings, with the most prominent location in the heart of the city. On the outside of the building was a huge sign on which the name of the firm was painted in large bold letters. Day after day as he passed by, a great dream took shape in the son's mind. He thought of how wonderful it would be if it was his family that had this great building – his family that owned and operated this great business.

One day as he stood gazing at the building, *in his imagination* he saw a completely different name on the huge sign across the entrance. Now the large letters spelled out *his family name* (in these case histories actual names are not used; for the sake of clarity in this story we will use hypothetical names and assume that the son's family name was Lordard). Where the sign read F. N. Moth & Co., *in imagination* he actually saw the name, letter by letter, J. N. Lordard & Sons. He remained looking at the sign with his eyes wide open, *imagining* that it read J. N. Lordard & Sons. Twice a day, week after week, month after month for two years he saw his family name over the front of that building. He was convinced that if he *felt strongly enough* that a thing was true, it was bound to be the case, and by *seeing in imagination* his family name on the sign – which implied that they owned the business – he became convinced that one day they *would* own it.

During this period, he told only one person what he was doing. He confided in his mother, who with loving concern tried to discourage him in order to protect him from what might be a great disappointment. Despite this, he persisted day after day. *Two years later the large company failed and the coveted building was up for sale.* On the day of the sale he seemed no nearer ownership than he had been two years before when he began to apply the law of assumption. During this period they had worked hard, and their customers had implicit confidence in them. However, they had not earned anything like the amount of money required for the purchase of the property. Nor did they have any source from which they could borrow the necessary capital. Making even more remote their chance of getting it was the fact that this was regarded as the most desirable property in the city and a number of wealthy business people were prepared to buy it. *On the actual day of the sale, to their complete surprise, a man, almost a total stranger, came into their shop and offered to buy the property for them.* (Due to some unusual conditions involved in this transaction the son's family could not even make a bid for the property.) They thought the man was joking. However, this was not the case. The man explained that he had watched them for some time, admired their ability, believed in their integrity, and that supplying the capital for them to go into business on a large scale was an extremely sound investment for him. *That very day the property was theirs.* What the son had persisted in seeing in his imagination was now a reality. The hunch of the stranger was more than justified. Today this family owns not only the particular business referred to but owns many of the largest industries in the country in which they live.

The son, *seeing his family name over the entrance of this great building, long before it was actually there, was using exactly the technique that produces results. By assuming the feeling that he already had what he desired – by making this a vivid reality in his imagination – by determined persistence, regardless of appearance or circumstance –, he inevitably caused his dream to become a reality.*

## 3

This is the story of a very unexpected result of an interview with a lady who came to consult me.

One afternoon a young grandmother, a business woman in New York, came to see me. She brought along her nine-year-old grandson, who was visiting her from his home in Pennsylvania. In response to her questions, I explained the law of assumption, describing in detail the procedure to be followed in attaining an objective. The boy sat quietly, apparently absorbed in a small toy truck while I explained to the grandmother the method of assuming the state of consciousness that would be hers were her desire already fulfilled. I told her the story of the soldier in camp who each night fell asleep, imagining himself to be in his own bed in his own home.

When the boy and his grandmother were leaving, he looked up at me with great excitement and said, "I know what I want and, now, I know how to get it." Surprised, I asked him what it was he wanted; he told me he had his heart set on a puppy. To this, the grandmother vigorously protested, telling the boy that it had been made clear repeatedly that he could not have a dog under any circumstances... that his father and mother would not allow it, that the boy was too young to care for it properly, and furthermore the father had a deep dislike for dogs – he actually hated to have one around.

All these were arguments the boy passionately desirous of having a dog, refused to understand. "Now I know what to do," he said. "Every night just as I am going off to sleep I am going to pretend that I have a dog and we are going for a walk." "No," said the grandmother, "that is not what Mr. Neville means. This was not meant for you. You cannot have a dog."

Approximately six weeks later, the grandmother told me, what was to her, an astonishing story. The boy's desire to own a dog was so intense that he had absorbed all that I had told his grandmother of how to attain one's desire – and he believed implicitly that at last he knew how to get a dog.

Putting this belief into practice, *for many nights the boy imagined a dog was lying in his bed beside him. In imagination he petted the dog actually feeling its fur.* Things like playing with the dog and taking it for a walk filled his mind.

Within a few weeks it happened. A newspaper in the city in which the boy lived organized a special program in connection with Kindness to Animals Week. All schoolchildren were requested to write an essay on "Why I Would Like to Own a Dog." After entries from all the schools were submitted and judged, the winner of the contest was announced.

The very same boy who weeks before in my apartment in New York had told me "Now I know how to get a dog" was the winner. In an elaborate ceremony, which was publicized with stories and pictures in the newspaper, the boy was awarded a beautiful *collie* puppy.

In relating this story, the grandmother told me that if the boy had been given the money with which to buy a dog, the parents would have refused to do so and would have used it to buy a bond for the boy or put it in the savings bank for him. Furthermore, if someone had made the boy a gift of a dog, they would have refused it or given it away. But the dramatic manner in which they boy got the dog, the way he won the city-wide contest, the stories and pictures in the newspaper, the pride of achievement and joy of the boy himself all combined to bring about a change of heart in the parents, and they found themselves doing that which they never conceived possible – they allowed him to keep the dog.

All this the grandmother explained to me, and she concluded by saying that there was one particular kind of dog on which the boy had set his heart. *It was a Collie.*

## 4

This was told by the Aunt in the story to the entire audience at the conclusion of one of my lectures.

During the question period following my lecture on the law of assumption, a lady who had attended many lectures and had had personal consultation with me on a number of occasions, rose and asked permission to tell a story illustrating how she had successfully used the law.

She said that upon returning home from the lecture the week before, she had found her niece distressed and terribly upset. The husband of the niece, who was an officer in the Army Air Force stationed in Atlantic City, had just been ordered, along with the rest of his unit, to active duty in Europe. She tearfully told her Aunt that the reason she was upset was that she had been hoping her husband would be assigned to Florida as an Instructor. They both loved Florida and were anxious to be stationed there and not to be separated. Upon hearing this story, the aunt stated that there was only one thing to do and that was to apply immediately the law of assumption. "Let's actualize it," she said. "If you were actually in Florida, what would you do? You would feel the warm breeze. You would smell the salt air. You would feel your toes sinking down into the sand. Well, let's do all that right now."

They took off their shoes and turning out the lights, *in imagination, they felt themselves actually in Florida feeling the warm breeze, smelling the sea air, pushing their toes into the sand.*

Forty-eight hours later the husband received a change of orders. His new instructions were to report immediately to Florida as an Air Force Instructor. Five days later, his wife was on a train to join him. While the Aunt, in order to help her niece to attain her desire, joined in with the niece in assuming the state of consciousness required, *she* did not go to Florida. That was not her desire. On the other hand, that was the *intense longing* of the niece.

## 5

This case is especially interesting because of the short interval of time between the application of this law of assumption and its visible manifestation.

A very prominent woman came to me in deep concern. She maintained a lovely city apartment and a large country home; but because the many demands made upon her were greater than her modest income, it was absolutely essential that she rent her apartment if she and her family were to spend the summer at their country home.

In previous years the apartment had been rented without difficulty early in the spring, but the day she came to me the rental season for summer sublets was over. The apartment had been in the hands of the best real estate agents for months, but no one had been interested even in coming to see it.

When she had described her predicament I explained how the law of assumption could be brought to bear on solving her problem. I suggested that by imagining the apartment had been rented by a person desiring immediate occupancy and by assuming that this was the case, her apartment actually would be rented. In order to create the necessary feeling of naturalness – the feeling that it was already a fact that her apartment was rented – I suggested that she drift off into sleep that very night imagining herself, *not in her apartment*, but in whatever place she would sleep were the apartment suddenly rented. She quickly grasped the idea and said that in such a situation she would sleep in her country home even though it was not yet opened for the summer.

This interview took place on Thursday. At nine o'clock the following Saturday morning she phoned me from her home in the country – excited and happy. She told me that on Thursday night *she had fallen asleep actually imagining and feeling that she was sleeping in her other bed in her country home many miles away from the city apartment she was occupying.* On Friday, the very next day, a highly desirable tenant, one who met all her requirements as a responsible person, not only rented the apartment, but rented it on the condition that he could move in that very day.

## 6

Only the most complete and intense use of the law of assumption could have produced such results in this extreme situation.

Four years ago a friend of our family asked that I talk with his twenty-eight-year old son who was not expected to live.

He was suffering from a rare heart disease. This disease resulted in a disintegration of the organ. Long and costly medical care had been of no avail. Doctors held out no hope for recovery. For a long time the son had been confined to his bed. His body had shrunk to almost a skeleton, and he could talk and breathe only with great difficulty. His wife and two small children were home when I called and his wife was present throughout our discussion.

I started by telling him that there was only one solution to any problem and that solution was a change of attitude. Since talking exhausted him, I asked him to nod in agreement if he understood clearly what I said. This he agreed to do. I described the facts underlying the law of consciousness – in fact that consciousness was the only reality. I told him that the way to change any condition was to change his state of consciousness concerning it. As a specific aid in helping him to assume the feeling of already being well, I suggested that in *imagination, he see the doctor's face expressing incredulous amazement in finding him recovered, contrary to all reason, from the last stages of an incurable disease, that he see him double checking in his examination and hear him saying over and over, "It's a miracle – it's a miracle."*

He not only understood all this clearly, but he believed it implicitly. He promised that he would faithfully follow this procedure. His wife, who had been listening intently, assured me that she, too, would diligently use the law of assumption and her imagination in the same way as her husband. The following day I sailed for New York – all this taking place during a winter vacation in the tropics. Several months later I received a letter saying the son had made a miraculous recovery. On my next visit I met him in person. He was in perfect health, actively engaged in business and thoroughly enjoying the many social activities of his friends and family.

He told me that from the day I left he never had any doubt that "it" would work. He described how he had faithfully followed the suggestion I had made to him and *day after day had lived completely in the assumption of already being well and strong.*

Now, four years after his recovery, he is convinced that the only reason he is here today is due to his successful use of the law of assumption.

## 7

This story illustrates the successful use of the law by a New York business executive.

In the fall of 1950 an executive of one of New York's prominent banks discussed with me a serious problem with which he was confronted. He told me that the outlook for his personal progress and advancement was very dim. Having reached middle age and feeling that a marked improvement in position and income was justified, he had "talked it out" with his superiors. They frankly told him that any major improvement was impossible and intimated that if he was dissatisfied he could seek another job. This, of course, only increased his uneasiness. In our talk he explained that he had no great desire for really big money but that he had to have a substantial income in order to maintain his home comfortably and to provide for the education of his children in good preparatory schools and colleges. This he found impossible on his present income. The refusal of the bank to assure him of any advancement in the near future resulted in a feeling of discontent and an intense desire to secure a better position with considerably more money. He confided in me that the kind of job he would like better than anything in the world was one in which he managed the investment funds of a large institution such as a foundation or great university.

In explaining the law of assumption, I stated that his present situation was only a manifestation of his concept of himself, and declared that if he wanted to change the circumstances in which he found himself, he could do so by changing his concept of himself. In order to bring about this change of consciousness, and thereby a change in his situation, I asked him to follow this procedure every night just before he fell asleep. *In imagination, he was to feel he was retiring at the end of one of the most important and successful days of his life. He was to imagine that he had actually closed a deal that very day to join the kind of organization he yearned to be with and in exactly the capacity he wanted.* I suggested to him that if he succeeded in completely filling his mind with this feeling, he would experience a definite sense of relief. In this mood his uneasiness and discontent would be a thing of the past. He would feel the contentment that comes with the fulfillment of desire. I wound up by assuring him that if he did this faithfully, he would inevitably get the kind of position he wanted.

This was the first week of December. *Night after night, without exception he followed this procedure.* Early in February a director of one of the wealthiest foundations in the world asked this executive if he would be interested in joining the foundation in an executive capacity handling investments. After some brief discussion he accepted.

Today at a substantially higher income and with the assurance of steady progress, this man is in a position far exceeding all that he had hoped for.

## 8

The man and wife in this story have attended my lectures for a number of years. It is an interesting illustration of the conscious use of this law by two people concentrating on the same objective at one time.

This man and wife were an exceptionally devoted couple. Their life was completely happy and entirely free from any problems or frustrations.

For some time, they had planned to move into a larger apartment. The more they thought about it, the more they realized that what they had their hearts set on was a beautiful penthouse. In discussing it together, the husband explained that he wanted one with a huge window looking out on a magnificent view. The wife said she would like to have one side of the walls mirrored from top to bottom. They both wanted to have a wood-burning fireplace. It was a "must" that the apartment be in New York City.

For months they had searched for just such an apartment in vain. In fact, the situation in the city was such that the securing of any kind of apartment was almost an impossibility. They were so scarce that not only were there waiting lists for them, but all sorts of special deals including premiums, the buying of furniture etc. were involved. New apartments were being leased long before they were completed, many being rented from the blueprints of the building.

Early in the spring after months of fruitless seeking, they finally located one which they seriously considered. It was a penthouse apartment in a building just being completed on upper Fifth Avenue facing Central Park.

It had one serious drawback. Being a new building, it was not subject to rent control and the couple felt the yearly rental was exorbitant. In fact, it was several thousand dollars a year more than they had considered paying. During the spring months of March and April, they continued looking at various penthouses throughout the city but they always came back to this one. Finally they decided to increase the amount they would pay substantially and made a proposition which the agent for the building agreed to forward to the owners for consideration.

It was at this point, without discussing it with each other, each determined to apply the law of assumption. It was not until later that each learned what the other had done. *Night after night, they both fell asleep in imagination in the apartment they were considering. The husband, lying with his eyes closed, would imagine that his bedroom windows were overlooking the park. He would imagine going to the window the first thing in the morning and enjoying the view. He felt himself sitting on the terrace overlooking the park, having cocktails with his wife and friends, all thoroughly enjoying it. He filled his mind with actually feeling himself in the penthouse and on the terrace. During all this time, unknown to him, his wife was doing the same thing.*

Several weeks went by without any decision on the part of the owners, but they continued to imagine as they fell asleep each night that they were actually sleeping in the penthouse.

One day, to their complete surprise, one of the employees in the apartment building in which they lived told them that the penthouse there was vacant. They were astonished because theirs was one of the most desirable buildings in the city with a perfect location right on Central Park. They knew there was a long waiting list of people trying to get an apartment in their building. The fact that a penthouse had unexpectedly become available was kept quiet by the management because they were not in a position to consider any applicants for it. Upon learning that it was vacant, this couple immediately made a request that it be rented to them, only to be told that this was impossible. The fact was that not only were there several people on a waiting list for a penthouse in the building but it was actually promised to one family. Despite this the couple had a series of meetings with the management, at the conclusion of which the apartment was theirs.

The building being subject to rent control, their rental was just about what they had planned to pay when they first started looking for a penthouse. The location, the apartment itself, and the large terrace surrounding it on the South, West, and North was beyond all their expectations – and in the living room on one *side is a giant window 15 feet by 8 feet with a magnificent view of Central Park; one wall is mirrored from floor to ceiling, and there is a wood-burning fireplace.*

# 24

# *Failure*

This book would not be complete without some discussion of failure in the attempted use of the law of assumption. It is entirely possible that you either have had or will have a number of failures in this respect – many of them in really important matters. If, having read this book, having a thorough knowledge of the application and working of the law of assumption, you faithfully apply it in an effort to attain some intense desire and fail, what is the reason? If to the question "Did you persist enough?" you can answer "Yes" – and still the attainment of your desire was not realized, what is the reason for failure?

The answer to this is the most important factor in the successful use of the law of assumption. *The time it takes your assumption to become fact, your desire to be fulfilled, is directly proportionate to the naturalness of your feeling of already being what you want to be – of already having what you desire.*

The fact that it does not feel *natural* to you to be what you imagine yourself to be is *the secret of your failure.* Regardless of your desire, regardless of how faithfully and intelligently you follow the law, if you do not feel *natural* about what you want to be, *you will not be it.* If it does not feel natural to you to get a better job, you will not get a better job. The whole principle is vividly expressed by the Bible phrase "you die in your sins" – you do not transcend from your present level to the state desired.

How can this feeling of naturalness be achieved? The secret lies in one word – imagination. For example, this is a very simple illustration. Assume that you are securely chained to a large heavy iron bench. You could not possibly run, in fact you could not even walk. In these circumstances it would not be natural for you to run. You could not even feel that it was natural for you to run. But you could easily *imagine* yourself running. In that instant, while your consciousness is filled with your *imagined* running, you have forgotten that you are bound. In *imagination* your running was completely natural.

The essential feeling of naturalness can be achieved by *persistently filling your consciousness with imagination* – imagining yourself being what you want to be or having what you desire.

Progress can spring only from your imagination, from your desire to transcend your present level. What you truly and literally must feel is that *with your imagination, all things are possible.* You must realize that changes are not caused by caprice, but by a change of consciousness. You may fail to achieve or sustain the particular state of consciousness necessary to produce the effect you desire. But, once you know that consciousness is the only reality and is the sole creator of your particular world and have burnt this truth into your whole being, then you know that success or failure is entirely in your own hands. Whether or not you are disciplined enough to sustain the required state of consciousness in specific instances has no bearing on the truth of the law itself – that an assumption, if persisted in, will harden into fact. The certainty of the truth of this law must remain despite great disappointment and tragedy – even when you "see the light of life go out and all the world go on as though it were still day." You must not believe that because your assumption failed to materialize, the truth that assumptions do materialize is a lie. If your assumptions are not fulfilled, it is because of some error or weakness in your consciousness. However, these errors and weaknesses *can be overcome.* Therefore, press on to the attainment of ever higher levels by feeling that you *already are* the person you want to be. And remember that the time it takes your assumption to become reality is *proportionate to the naturalness of being it.*

> "Man surrounds himself with the true image of himself. Every spirit builds itself a house and beyond its house a world, and beyond its world a heaven. Know then that the world exists for you. For you the phenomenon is perfect. What we are, that only can we see. All that Adam had, all that Caesar could, you have and can do. Adam called his house, heaven and earth. Caesar called his house, Rome; you perhaps call yours a cobbler's trade; a hundred acres of land, or a scholar's garret. Yet line for line and point for point, your dominion is as great as theirs, though without fine name. Build therefore your own world. As fast as you conform your life to the pure idea in your mind, that will unfold its great proportion."
>
> EMERSON

# 25

# *Faith*

> "A miracle is the name given, by those who have no faith, to the works of faith."
>
> "Faith is the substance of things hoped for, the evidence of things not seen."
>
> HEBREWS 11:1

The very reason for the law of assumption is contained in this quotation. If there were not a deep seated awareness that that which you hope for had substance and was possible of attainment it would be impossible to assume the consciousness of being or having it. It is the fact that *creation is finished and everything exists that stirs you to hope* – and hope, in turn, *implies expectation,* and without expectation of success it would be impossible to use consciously the law of assumption. "Evidence" is a sign of actuality. Thus, this quotation means that *faith is the awareness of the reality of that which you assume.* Consequently, it is obvious that a lack of faith means disbelief in the existence of that which you desire. Inasmuch as that which you experience is the faithful reproduction of your state of consciousness, lack of faith will mean perpetual failure in any *conscious* use of the law of assumption.

In all the ages of history faith has played a major role. It permeates all the great religions of the world, it is woven all through mythology and yet, today, it is almost universally misunderstood.

Contrary to popular opinion, the efficacy of faith is not due to the work of any outside agency. It is from first to last *an activity of your own consciousness.*

The Bible is full of many statements about faith, of the true meaning of which few are aware. Here are some typical examples:

> "Unto us was the gospel preached, as well as unto them: but the word preached did not profit them, not being mixed with faith in them that heard it."
>
> HEBREWS 4:2

In this quotation, the 'us' and 'them' make clear that all of us hear the gospel. "Gospel" means 'good news'. Very obviously good news for you would be that you had attained your desire. This is always being 'preached' to you by your infinite self. To hear that which you desire does exist and you need only to accept it in consciousness is good news. Not "mixing with faith" means to deny the reality of that which you desire. Hence there is no "profit" (attainment) possible.

> "O faithless and perverse generation, how long shall I be with you."
>
> MATTHEW 17:17

The meaning of "faithless" has been made clear. "Perverse" means turned the wrong way, in other words, the consciousness of *not* being what you want to be. To be faithless, that is, to disbelieve in the reality of that which you assume, is to be perverse. "How long shall I be with you" means that the fulfillment of your desire is *predicated upon your change to the right state of consciousness.* It is just as though that which you desire is telling you that it will not be yours until you turn from being faithless and perverse to righteousness. As already stated, righteousness is the consciousness of already being what you want to be.

> "By faith he forsook Egypt, not fearing the wrath of the king: for he endured, as seeing him who is invisible."
>
> HEBREWS 11:27

"Egypt" means darkness, belief in many gods (causes). The "king" symbolizes the power of outside conditions or circumstances. "He" is your concept of yourself as already being what you want to be. "Enduring as seeing him who is invisible" means persisting in the assumption that your desire is *already* fulfilled. Thus this quotation means that by persisting in the assumption that you already are the person you want to be, you rise above all doubt, fear, and belief in the power of outside conditions or circumstances; and your world inevitably conforms to your assumption.

The dictionary definitions of faith:

> "the ascent of the mind or understanding to the truth" –
> "unwavering adherence to principle"

are so pertinent that they might well have been written with the law of assumption in mind.

Faith does not question – Faith knows.

26

# *Destiny*

Your destiny is that which you must inevitably experience. Really it is an infinite number of individual destinies, each of which when attained is the starting place for a new destiny.

Since life is *infinite,* the concept of an ultimate destiny is inconceivable. When we understand that consciousness is the only reality, we know that it is the only creator. This means that your consciousness is the creator of your destiny. The fact is, you are creating your destiny every moment, *whether you know it or not.* Much that is good and even wonderful has come into your life without your having any inkling that you were the creator of it.

However, the understanding of the causes of your experience, and the *knowledge that you are the sole creator of the contents of your life, both good and bad, not only make you a much keener observer of all phenomena, but through the awareness of the power of your own consciousness, intensify your appreciation of the richness and grandeur of life.*

Regardless of occasional experiences to the contrary, it is *your destiny to rise to higher and higher states of consciousness, and to bring into manifestation more and more of creation's infinite wonders.* Actually, you are destined to reach the point where you realize that through your own desire you can consciously create your successive destinies.

The study of this book, with its detailed exposition of consciousness and the operation of the law of assumption, is the master key to the conscious attainment of your highest destiny.

This very day start your new life. Approach every experience in a new frame of mind – with a new state of consciousness. Assume the noblest and the best for yourself in every respect and continue therein.

Make believe – great wonders are possible.

# 27

# *Reverence*

> "Never wouldst Thou have made anything if Thou hadst not loved it."
>
> **Wisdom 11:24**

In all creation, in all eternity, in all the realms of your infinite being, the most wonderful fact is that which is stressed in the first chapter of this book. *You are God.* You are the "I am that I am". You are consciousness. You are the creator. This is the mystery, this is the great secret known by the seers, prophets and mystics throughout the ages. This is the truth that you can never know *intellectually*. Who is this you? That it is you, John Jones or Mary Smith, is absurd. It is the consciousness which knows that you are John Jones or Mary Smith. It is your greater self, your deeper self, your infinite being. Call it what you will. The important thing is that *it is within you, it is you, it is your world.* It is this fact that underlies the immutable law of assumption. It is upon this fact that your very existence is built. It is this fact that is the foundation of every chapter of this book. No, you cannot know this intellectually, you cannot debate it, you cannot substantiate it. *You can only feel it. You can only be aware of it.*

Becoming aware of it, one great emotion permeates your being. You live with a perpetual feeling of *reverence*. The knowledge that your creator is the very self of yourself and never would have made you had he not *loved you* must fill your heart with devotion, yes, with adoration. One knowing glimpse of the world about you at any single instant of time is sufficient to fill you with profound awe and a feeling of worship.

It is when your feeling of reverence is most intense that you are closest to God, and *when you are closest to God your life is richest.*

> "Our deepest feelings are precisely those we are least able to express, and even in the act of adoration, silence is our highest praise."

5

# The Secret of Imagining

# *The Secret of Imagining*

In almost every particular is the world about us different from what we think it. Why then should we be so incredulous? Life calls on us to believe not less, but more. The secret of imaging is the greatest of all problems, to the solution of which everyone should aspire, for supreme power, supreme wisdom, supreme delight lie in the solution of this mystery.

If you have solved the mystery of imagining you have found Jesus Christ. Jesus Christ is defined for us in scripture as "The power of God and the wisdom of God" (First Corinthians 1:24). As we are told in the eighth chapter of the Book of Proverbs,—and Wisdom is speaking now, personified as a little child:

> *"When He laid out the foundation of the world*
> *I was beside Him like a little child*
> *I was daily His delight,*
> *rejoicing before Him always*
> *rejoicing in His inhabited world,*
> *delighting in the affairs of men.*
> *He who finds me finds life*
> *He who misses me injures himself;*
> *All who hate me love death."*

**Proverbs 8:29-31, 35, 36**

So find that child that is the symbol of Jesus Christ, who is the creative power and the wisdom of God. Believe me when I tell you that this Jesus Christ of scripture is your own wonderful human imagination. "By him all things were made, and without him was not anything made that was made" (John 1:3). He is in the world, and the world was made by Him, and the world knows Him not.

Look into the world and name one thing that wasn't first imagined. You name one thing that does not now exist in your imagination—just name it. Name anything in the world that does not now exist in your imagination: "All things exist in the human imagination." (from "Jerusalem" by William Blake)

"God is man, and exists in us and we in Him" (from "Annotations to Berkeley" by William Blake). The eternal abode of man is the imagination; and that is God Himself. Try to disprove it.

God is my pure imagining in myself. He underlies all of my faculties, including perception, but He streams into my surface mind least disguised in the form of productive fancy. I can catch Him in the act of producing these images in my mind. Just try it as you are seated here. Try to think of anything. Try to catch Him in the act of actually producing in your own mind's eye all these images. "For all things exist in the human imagination." But how can I single out one and clothe it so that it becomes an objective fact?

That is the secret, for they all exist within me. But how can I catch one and clothe it? Well I will try to show you tonight what I know from my own personal experience. Scripture teaches it, but it tells it in a strange and wonderful way: how to clothe it.

You see this room in which we are now? It's more real now than your own home is to you; yet you know your home more intimately than you know this room. Yet this room, at the moment, while you are in it, is more real than your own home. How different the cubic reality from the plane of any depiction of it. This room is now so "real" because we are in it, and we are all imagination. We're in it; and to us, it's real. Think of your own home. Do we not have the capacity to draw it, to paint it? But in your mind's eye you have a plane depiction of it, but it's not as real now as the room is. This room is real because we're in it.

Now this is what I mean by making something that is only a thought—something that is real. How do I do it? I single out, out of my own wonderful human imagination, that which I want to make real. It's all in you. Then I must enter into it as I have entered into this room. "If the spectator would enter into any one of these images in his imagination, approaching it on the fiery chariot of his own contemplative thought" (from "Visions of the Last Judgment" by William Blake), it would become just as real to him as this room.

You may ask, "What would that do to me? Will it become real in the not-distant future?" I know from my own experience, it will. You can sit here and enter into a state. It may not take on quite the reality of this room, but it will if you persist in it; it will become just like this. When you open your eyes, it vanishes. But does it mean that I tasted that, and that's all? No. Having gone into it, may I tell you, it will follow you? It will not recede into the past as memory; it will advance into the future and you will confront it. This is the secret of imaging, which is finding out the secret of God.

You are an immortal being. You cannot die because you are all imagination. Man is all imagination; and God truly is man; and He exists in us, and we in Him. And that immortal body of man is the human imagination, and that is Jesus Christ Himself,—the Eternal Body of man and it cannot die. You cannot die. The body,—yes, this will fade; but I am not the garment that I am wearing. I am the wearer of the garment, and the wearer of this garment is all imagination. This is the story that the Bible teaches.

When we read in the Bible: "I, even I, am He. I kill, and I make alive; I wound, and I heal; and there is no god beside me" (Deuteronomy 32:39). This is not a being outside of you speaking; this is the Being that you really are, speaking within you, trying to persuade Himself of His own wonderful power to create. It can kill, and yet it can make alive. It can resurrect from the dead. And that is your own wonderful human imagination.

The day will come; you will taste this power that you possess. You will come into a room just like this, and you will still it—not by commanding anyone in the room to be still. Leave them just as they are. But you will arrest within yourself an activity that you feel, and as you still it in you, everything that you observe becomes still—perfectly still. You could go forward and examine them, and they are dead. Everything is perfectly still and dead. The life is in you. You release the activity, and they once more become animated and continue to do what they intended to do. You could, when you stilled the activity within you, change their motivation; and when you release it, they will do entirely different from what they intended to do prior to your arrestment within you of that activity.

"As the Father has life in Himself, He has granted the Son also to have life in Himself" (John 5:26); and you have that within you. You're not quite aware of it yet, but you will become aware. Those that I am teaching will have dreams, as you have dreams; and in their dreams they will become awake, and then arrest it in the dream and change the motivation and see the intended act change.

Here is one. A friend became aware that she was dreaming, and here's a man who intended to hurt her. He got out of the car and came towards her, and she became afraid; and her fright woke her; but instead of walking on the bed, she awoke in the dream. Then she realized, "This is what he teaches. Now I will simply arrest it." She didn't argue with him; she arrested, within her, the activity that animated him. And she said to him, "You are tired. You need a good hot cup of coffee and then a good sound sleep," and then she told him exactly what he needed, and released the activity within her. He shook his head as though something strange had happened within him, and he got back into the car—all in her dream—and drove off. You see, she changed his intention towards her.

This may seem impossible to the world. As I started this lecture, almost everything in this world is so completely unlike what it appears to be. And I am telling you from my own experience; I am not speculating. I am not theorizing. The power of which I speak is a power within you. That power is not something on the outside; it's your own wonderful human imagination, and you will learn to control it. Your imagination animates the world in which you live. You change your imagination, and you change the world.

To attempt to change circumstances before I change my own imaginal activity is to struggle against the very nature of my own being, for my own imaginal activity is animating my world. If I believe that I am injured or that others are against me, I have conjured them in my world, and they have to be against me. If I fully believe that all are working towards the fulfilment of my good, they have to work towards the fulfilment of my good. I don't ask them. I don't compel them. I simply do it only within myself, and the whole vast world exists within me. Therefore, it is myself "pushed out." It's objectified. I don't have to change affairs; I only change it within myself; and then everyone, though I know him or not by name,—it doesn't really matter,—it's myself "pushed out."

I couldn't tell you the atoms of my body, but it is my body. I couldn't tell you if you took the handoff that it's my hand I am looking at, any more than I could tell you your name or anything about you; yet, you are myself "pushed out," as this body is the body I wear. And so, as the body obeys my mind, you—my "pushed-out" body—will obey my mind too. All I have to do is to concern myself with what I want in this world, and try to keep it within the frame of the Golden Rule; doing unto others only that which I would want done unto me,—nothing more than that; hurting no one, doing not a thing to anyone other than that which I would want done unto me.

If you want all the lovely things done,—do only the lovely, and do it all in your own wonderful human imagination. Then you will realize this tremendous secret of imaging. It is the greatest of all secrets, to the solution of which everyone in the world should aspire, because Christ is the answer.

Christ is defined for us in the first chapter of First Corinthians as "the power of God and the wisdom of God" (First Corinthians 1:24). Here is the power of God and the wisdom of God; and I have found the power to be in myself.

"You mean, Christ is in me?" Are we not taught that in scripture? "Know ye not that Jesus Christ is in you? Do you not know that Jesus Christ is in you, unless of course you fail to meet the test?" (Second Corinthians 13:5) Well then, test it. How would I test it?

A friend of mine, maybe, is unwell; or maybe he's unemployed, or maybe he is not earning enough to meet the obligations of life. All right, he is in me. As I think of him, he's in me. He need not be physically present for me to think of him; he's in me. I think of him; I conjure him. Well, can I change his entire picture in me? I assume that he is talking to me, and he's telling me that he has never had more, he has never felt better; and as I believe in what I am seeing in my own mind's eye,—I believe in him. That is Christ in me, and all things are possible to Christ. Well then, test it and see if it works. See if you do not see him in the not-distance future earning more, looking better; and everything in the world that you have done within you, he responds to. He need not praise you or thank you. You don't need his praise; you don't need his thanks. You don't need confirmation from him, other than he does conform to what you have done in yourself concerning him.

You ask no one to thank you. Thank nothing. You are simply exercising the power of God within you. "And the power of God and the wisdom of God is Jesus Christ" (First Corinthians 1:24). And there is nothing in the world but God. It is all God in you "pushed out," and God is your own wonderful human imagination. He can't be closer. God is never so far off as even to be near, for nearness implies separation. He's not separated. God actually, literally became as I AM, that I may be as He is. He is not something on the outside. No matter how near He is, He can't even touch me. He actually became me, with all of my weaknesses, all of my limitations; and now I am trying to struggle within myself to find out who I AM,—and that's His name. My name is in Him. What's your name? "Go and say I AM has sent you." "Is that you name?" "Yes, forever and forever it is my name." "What name? Jehovah?" "No." "The Lord?" "No, I AM." That's His name. That is His name forever and forever.

Well I cannot say, "I AM," and point elsewhere. I can't say, "I AM," and feel something is near me. It can't even be near. Something can be near to what I AM, but "I AM" can't be near. And that's the name of God forever and forever. So you are the Lord Jesus Christ.

Now a pattern is given to us in scripture by which you will know that you are; and I promise you, from my own personal experience, that you shall have it. It is a true story. The truest story ever told is the story of the Lord Jesus Christ. When He said, "I AM the Father," may I tell you, if he's a father, he has a son, hasn't he? Or at least he has a child; but I tell you, it's a son. He said, "When you see me, you see the Father"; but if I look at you and I say, "Well then, you are the father, show me your son." He can't show me His son outside as His son, because He and I are one. He has to show me His son not of blood nor of the will of the flesh; it has to be born, not of blood nor of the will of the flesh nor of the will of man, but of God. And He tells me that He is God, and He tells me that He and I are one. Well then, it can't be born in any normal, natural way. He has to be born of God.

Well then, who is your son? He tells me in scripture that David calls Him, "Father."

"David calls you, 'Father'?"

"Yes." He said, "I inspired the prophets," and read the Prophets; and in the Prophets, David calls the Lord, "my Father."

"You mean, David, then, is my son?"

"Yes, he's my son."

"But I do not know him," you will say.

But I will tell you, from my own personal experience, you will know it because I know it; David called me, "my Father." David called me, "my Lord." David called me the Rock of his salvation. Everything that is said in scripture concerning what he said of the Lord, he said of me. And so, I stood, and here is David, and I knew it beyond all doubt that here is my son, and my son is David,—not a David,—the David—the only David—

the David of biblical fame. And as he called me, "Father," memory returned.

So God actually became me, and then He unfolds Himself within me. Well, as He unfolds Himself within me, it's only the memory of God that He gave up in order to become me. He had to completely give up all that was God to become this little witness that is called a man called Neville. So when His memory returns and He became me, it is my memory returning. He actually gave me Himself as He gave you Himself; and the day will come as He unfolds Himself within you, your memory returns because it's God's memory returning. He completely empties Himself in order to become you.

This is the story of the Christian faith; the fulfilment of all the promises made in the Old Testament. The Old Testament is only a prophetic blueprint of the life of Jesus Christ. It's an adumbration, a foreshadowing in a not-altogether conclusive or immediately evident way; but as it unfolds within you, it's nothing more than God's memory returning. But having become you, it becomes your memory returning, and you awaken as God Himself. And there is nothing in the world like God.

Now you ask, what, all the horrors of the world, the pain, the suffering? Yes. It takes all the "furnaces" to prepare you to receive the gift that He gives, and the gift is Himself. God actually became you. He gave Himself to you, that you may be God. And God in you is your own wonderful human imagination, that's God.

Now tonight try it. I ask you to believe me. But whether you believe me or not, try it anyway. Take a friend of yours and bring him before your mind's eye, and then talk to him from the premise of your desire for him fulfilled—not going to be, but already fulfilled. And having done it, believe that all things are possible to the Lord Jesus Christ; and you just saw Jesus Christ in action, for you saw the creative power of God in action, and that's Jesus Christ. That is your own wonderful human imagination.

Now believe in the reality of what you've just done. Believe that this subjective appropriation of your objective hope for a friend is a fact. That is really praying. And all things are possible to God. Go within and appropriate it—just completely appropriate it, and see it unfold within your own vast marvellous world.

So this wonderful secret is the secret of the Lord Jesus Christ. If you turn on the outside and turn to another, you do not know the Lord Jesus Christ. You can make all kinds of images of Him. That's not the Lord Jesus Christ. If any man should ever come and say, "Look, there he is," or "Here he is," don't believe it. Why? Because when you actually meet Him, you are going to meet your Self. The Christ of faith comes to us as one unknown; yet one who in some ineffable mystery lets us experience who He is; and when we experience Jesus Christ, we experience Him in the first-person, singular, present-tense experience. You will never see Him coming from without. Let no one tell you you're going to meet Him coming from without. You will meet Him awakening Himself within you as you. That's the Lord Jesus Christ. That's the great sacrifice. He is crucified on Humanity.

Every human form is the cross that He wears; and in that form He awakens as the one in whom He awakens. He awakens as that Being, and that Being is the Lord Jesus Christ. And because He is the father of David, David called that Being, "Father"; then you know, "I AM He."

Oh, I can tell you from now to the ends of time, and I may not persuade you to believe it; but when it happens to you, you need no further persuasion, for you are confronted with the facts and there you stand in the presence of you own son, and the son is the Son of God.

"I will tell of the decree of the Lord," said David. "He said unto me, 'Thou art my son. Today I have begotten thee.'" (Psalm 2:7) These are the words of David in the Second Psalm. "I will tell of the decree of the Lord. He said unto me, 'Thou art my son.'" That son is going to call you, "Father"; and then, and only then, you will know you are God the Father. That is the mystery of the entire world. And so, what you accomplish in this world concerning finances is wonderful for you as an individual in the world of Caesar. What you do concerning the social world—all these things—it's marvellous; but you will only really fulfil your destiny as you fulfil scripture, for the purpose of life is to fulfil scripture.

"I have accomplished the work Thou gavest me to do." What work? All that the prophets spoke about me; and beginning with Moses and the prophets and the Psalms; he interpreted to them in all the scriptures the things concerning Himself. Then said he, "Scripture must be fulfilled in you," and the purpose of life is to fulfil scripture—the prophecy of God to man, for He gave man Himself, or promised to give man Himself. And He promised me a son. The son He promised was His Son; and in giving me His Son, He gave me Himself, for His Son calls me, "Father." And that is the whole mystery of life. There's nothing but God. One Being expanding Himself forever and forever and forever, each Himself. And even though he calls you, "Father," may I tell you, you will not lose your identity. You are individualized and you will tend towards ever greater and greater individualization. And yet, you are the Father of my son; and if you are the Father of my son, then you and I are one. It is a great mystery,—we are brothers,—for you do not lose your identity and I do not lose my identity. So you and I, behind these masks are eternal brothers—the Father of the One and only Begotten Son.

Well if you are the father of my son, and my own wife is the "father" of my son, then the relationship on earth of men, or friend to friend and wife to husband, is above this level, and we are eternal brothers, all forming the one Father.

So tonight, you take me seriously; and when you go home—or start it here,—you put into practice this greatest of all secrets; the secret of imaging. There is no greater secret in the world. Every child born of woman is alive because it was imagined. And imaging is God in action. That's the soul of man—imaging; and that is the power of God. And the power of God is Christ. And that is the wisdom of God, and the wisdom of God is Christ.

A child can imagine. Well, that's Christ. That is Christ crucified on that little tiny garment, and it suffers with everything that that little child imagines, or it enjoys with everything the little child imagines. It wears all the stripes and all the blows that man in his misuse of that power will do. He doesn't criticize him. He waits upon me as indifferently—and as quickly—

when the will in me is evil as when it is good. That way, He bears all my stripes. He bears all of my misuse of His power, knowing that in the end, I will awaken and use it only lovingly.

When I completely awaken from the dream of life, I will use this creative power of God only lovingly. But in the meantime while I am trying to awaken to the use of this power, I misuse it. And may I tell you, you will confront this vision, and you will see what you did from the beginning, for you didn't begin it a few years ago in your mother's womb. You have been coming through the centuries.

One night, here I saw this monstrous creature covered in hair. It looked like a gorilla, and the hair was all dark brown from head to toe. It was a monster. And here, the most glorious, heavenly creature—a female; and this was a male monster. And it called out to this heavenly creature, "Mother, mother." Well, I knew this could not be—this radiant, heavenly creature; and so I struck him. And as I struck it, it gloated; it loved violence. And I pummelled it, and it gloated all the more. Well, it could speak in a guttural tone, calling this heavenly being, "Mother." And that annoyed me. Then suddenly from within me I knew. Why, this is my own creation. And so is this one. They are only the out picturing of my two different uses of the creative power that I AM.

Here (the monster) is the complete embodiment of every misused moment of my life. Every time I was violent, I created and fed this monster. It whispered in my ear to be monstrous, to be violent, to be bad, to be evil, for it fed only on this thought. And here (the heavenly creature) was the embodiment of all my loving thoughts. Every kind, considerate, wonderful thought in my life fed this one.

As I saw this monstrous thing and realized that it was my own offspring,—it was the fruit of my misspent energy,—I pledged myself. There was no one to whom I could turn,—I pledged myself that if it took eternity I would redeem it. It did not come into being through any power other than my own misuse of my own power. It could not have been brought into being; and that thing could not live, and it could not help itself. I didn't condemn it.

At that moment, I felt compassion beyond the wildest dreams of anyone for this monstrous thing that I had created. And when I made myself that pledge that I would redeem it if it took me eternity, at that very moment, the whole thing got smaller and smaller and smaller; but it didn't waste—the energy that it embodied returned to me. I began to feel a power that, until that moment, I had never felt before. And this one began to grow. The beauty that she embodied and personified glowed as the energy came back from this one (the monster) to me; and the whole thing dissolved before my eyes.

So, "nothing is lost in all my holy mountain" I did not lose that energy that I misplaced,—it returned to me,—that was embodied in that monster. And throughout the centuries, it was it who whispered in my ear monstrous things to be done, because it could only feed on violence. It could only feed on evil.

Then I realized what it meant: that I ate of the Tree of the Knowledge of Good and Evil. And so it fed upon evil, and she fed upon the good. And then the evil that was only the energy misspent returned to me; and then the whole thing came back to me. And then I broke the spell, and I awoke in this world.

Well everyone is going to confront that gorilla on the threshold. Everyone has him, unseen by mortal eye, and he whispers into your ear to entertain the unlovely thoughts of the world. And your every reaction that is unlovely, it feeds upon it; and your every thought that is kind and wonderful and loving, she feeds upon it. And the day will come, you will be strong enough to confront this. And may I tell you, it will take you the twinkling of a second to dissolve it? You don't labor upon it. All it needs is the core of integrity within you. When you pledge yourself, and no one else,—you don't swear upon your mother, you don't swear upon a friend, you don't swear upon the Bible; you pledge yourself to redeem it. At the moment you pledge yourself,—and within you, you know you mean it,—the whole thing dissolves. It's no time at all in dissolving. And then all the energy returns to you, and you are stronger than ever before to go forward now and eat of the Tree of the Knowledge of Good and Evil.

And if you forward and misuse it again, you start another form building; and one day you will dissolve it again. Eventually you will become completely awakened, and you will use your wonderful power only—not for good,—that tree will come to an end,—for Life itself. For eating of the Tree of the Knowledge of Good and Evil is this world. The day will come that you will eat of the Tree of Life that bears the fruit of truth and error. Error will embody itself here, and one day you will confront the error, and the error will dissolve before your mind's eye as truth begins to glow before you, because you are eating, then, of the Tree of Life as you formally ate of the Tree of the Knowledge of Good and Evil. And the combat of good and evil produces this monster, and the combat of truth and error produces an entirely different form of being, more glorious than that one of good and more horrible than this. The error will dissolve just as quickly when you confront error.

So if today your teaching is not true and you live by it, you are building something just as monstrous; but one day you will confront error and you will discover that you lived by a false concept of God—something on the outside of Self; that you formerly worshiped a little golden figure made of gold and silver. It had eyes, but could not see. It had ears, but could not hear. It had a mouth, but could not speak. It had feet, and it could not walk. It made no sound within its throat. And those who made it are just like it. And those who trusted it are just like it too.

So all the little icons in the world that people worship—these are the little things called "error"; and one day you will discover the true God. And when you discover the true God, you will find that He is all within your own wonderful being as your own wonderful human imagination. You'll walk in the consciousness of being God. You don't brag about it.

As Blake answered when they asked him, "What do you think of Jesus Christ?" Blake answered, "Jesus Christ is the only God"; but he hastened to add to it, "But so am I, and so are you."

So you don't tell anyone. You simply know that you are the Being spoken of in scripture as "God the Father." For all that is said of Him, you are going to experience; and you are going to experience it in the first-person, singular, and a present-tense experience. And then you will know.

Today is the eleventh year since it happened to me right here in this city, right across the way at the hotel with the star at the top of the roof, the Sir Francis Drake, on the 20th day of July 1959. It was then that I, at 4:00 in the morning, felt within my head the most intense vibration, and I thought, this is a brain hemorrhage, and this is it. I knew nothing of the human form, and I thought I cannot possible survive what I am feeling; so this must be what they call a massive brain hemorrhage. But instead of departing this world, I awoke to find myself within my own skull; and I knew that I was entombed completely within my own skull. I was fully awake, as I've never been awake before, and here I am sealed—the skull is sealed, and I AM in it. The skull is not a little thing like this (indicating the head). It's the size of a huge, big sepulcher, and I knew it to be my skull. I also know intuitively that I could get out by pushing the base of my skull. As I pushed it, a stone rolled away, and I saw the little opening, and I put my head through it and pushed; and I came out, inch by inch, just as a child is born from the mother's womb. But instead of being born from below of flesh and blood, I was "born from above" out of the skull—Golgotha, where Christ was buried. But it was not another coming out,—I am coming out. There was no other. I had no companion in that skull. I myself was there, and I came out. And when I looked back at the body out of which I came, it was ghastly pale, turning its head from side to side like one in recovery from a great ordeal. I stood up and looked at it, and then suddenly I heard this strange, strange wind—this unearthly wind that I had heard in the tomb within my head,—well now, it seemed to be divided and coming from the corner of the room.

As I looked over to see if it really came from that side, and I looked back three or four seconds later the body had been removed. There is no body; but in its place sat my three older brothers. My eldest sat where the head was, my second one sat where the right foot was, and the third one sat where the left foot was; and they heart this same unearthly wind. They couldn't see me. I not only saw them, I could read their thoughts as

I could read my own. Their thoughts all were objective to me. Everything was objective. They couldn't have an emotion that wasn't objective. They couldn't have a thought that wasn't objective. And yet, I heard their voices.

And then my brother Lawrence got off the bed and started towards the same direction that I thought this wind originated—this peculiar wind. As he took one or two steps, he said, "Why, it's Neville's baby. This is the cause of this peculiar, unearthly wind."

My brother Victor and my brother Cecil, they said, "How can Neville have a baby?"

He didn't argue the point. He lifted from the floor a little infant wrapped in swaddling clothes and brought it and placed it on the bed; and I took that infant up into my arms, and as I looked into its face and said, "How is my sweetheart," this little heavenly face broke into the most glorious smile; and then the whole scene dissolved.

There was the resurrection from the dead, followed by the "birth from above." So we are "born from above," as told us in the Book of Peter. "We are born anew through the resurrection of Jesus Christ from the dead." (First Peter 1:3) There is only one Being resurrected, the Being who descended into man; and that is Jesus Christ. He descended into man, the power of God and the wisdom of God, and united with man; and when they became one and fulfilled the destiny of that Being, only He now wakes as you. And so, you awake as the Lord Jesus Christ, without loss of identity.

So eleven years ago on the 20th day of July, back in 1959 here in this city, that drama took place within me. So it is my birthday today in a spiritual sense. The little body that now stands before you, that came in the year 1905. It will depart and turn into dust; but that which awoke within me is the Immortal Self that cannot die. And those who have not had the experience, that Immortal Self is still there, and it cannot die. You will be restored to life in a world just like this to continue the drama until that experience that I've just told you takes place within you.

Nothing dies. The little rose that bloomed once, blooms forever. It turns to ash as the body will turn to ash, but you—the Immortal You, who is all imagination—cannot die. But it will awaken one day in the same manner that it awoke within me. It was buried in Golgotha, which means "the skull." He is buried on Calvary, which is the skull. It is in the skull of man that God is buried; and there God-in-man will awake.

So here this night you put it to the test as you are challenged in scripture to test Him. And you test, not another, you test your own wonderful human imagination, for that is the Lord Jesus Christ.

The truest story ever told is the story of Jesus Christ. Let the world rise in opposition and say there is no Lord. As Blake brought out so beautifully in his poem "Jerusalem":

"...Babel mocks; saying there is no God or Son of God;

That Thou, O Human Imagination, O Divine Body of the Lord Jesus Christ art all A delusion; but I know Thee, O Lord, when Thou arisest upon My weary eyes, even in this dungeon and this iron mill...

For Thou also sufferest with me, although I behold Thee not.

...And the Divine Voice answers,

...Fear not. Lo, I AM with you always,

Only believe in me, that I have the power to raise from death Thy Brother who sleepeth in Albion."

You can't get away from your own imagination. You can't get away from it because that's your own being. That is the reality. But it suffers with you. He is the Lord Jesus Christ within you. Now test Him tonight. Test Him for the good. Do you want a better job when they say they are letting people out? Forget what the papers say. Forget what anything says. "All things are possible to the Lord Jesus Christ." (Matthew 19:26)

If you don't have enough money, forget what the paper says, you assume that you have it. "All things are possible to God." He sets no limits whatsoever on the power of believing. Can you believe it? We'll try to believe it. Try to believe, first of all, in God. Well God is your own imagination. Well believe in Him; that whatever you can imagine is possible.

Can you imagine that you have now the kind of a job that you want? The income that would come from it? The fun in the doing of the work?

Well then walk as though it were true; and to the best of your ability believe that it's true. And that assumption though denied by your senses,—though the world would say it is false; if you persist in it, it will harden into fact. This is the law of your own wonderful imaging. Believe it, and it will become a reality.

# *About the Author*

Neville Goddard is well known as one of the most influential teachers and writers of metaphysical work. Neville was born on 19 February, 1905 in Barbados. He was the fourth child in a family of nine boys and one girl. In 1922, Neville came to the United States to study drama at the age of seventeen. During his entertaining tour in England as a vaudeville dancer and stage actor, he developed a great interest in metaphysics. Hence, he gave up his entertainment job and devote fully to the study of metaphysics and spiritual matters. Neville gives the readers the necessary tools to understand and manifest what they desire in their lives.

# HARDCOVER NON-FICTION

- 12 Years A Slave by Solomon Northup, ISBN: 9789354993985
- 51 Must Know Facts About Albert Einstein by GP Editors, ISBN: 9789354992285
- 51 Must Know Facts About Brain by GP Editors, ISBN: 9789354994654
- A Theory of Human Motivation by A.H. Maslow, ISBN: 9789354994005
- Becoming a Writer by Dorothea Brande, ISBN: 9789389157192
- Believe in Yourself by Joseph Murphy, ISBN: 9789388118439
- Beyond Good and Evil by Friedrich Nietzsche, ISBN: 9789389157871
- Chanakya Neeti by Chanakya, ISBN: 9789390492916
- Creative Mind and Success by Ernest Holmes, ISBN: 9789354991141
- Feeling is the Secret by Neville Goddard, ISBN: 9789389157208
- Five Chimneys by Olga Lengyel, ISBN: 9789354994043
- Five Lessons by Neville Goddard, ISBN: 9789354994050
- Gravity by George Gamow, ISBN: 9789388118705
- Great Speeches of Abraham Lincoln, ISBN: 9789387669154
- How to Attract Money by Joseph Murphy, ISBN: 9789388118446
- How to Develop Self Confidence and... by Dale Carnegie, ISBN: 9789388118286
- How to Enjoy Your Life and Your Job by Dale Carnegie, ISBN: 9789388118293
- How to Own Your Own Mind by Napoleon Hill, ISBN: 9789354994067
- How to Stop Worrying and Start Living by Dale Carnegie, ISBN: 9789387669161
- How to Win Friends and Influ. People by Dale Carnegie, ISBN: 9789387669178
- If You Want to Write by Brenda Ueland, ISBN: 9789389157895
- Illustrated Bio. of William Shakespeare by Manju Gupta, ISBN: 9789387669246
- Life in Corona by NK Sondhi, ISBN: 9789354994081
- Madhubala by Manju Gupta, ISBN: 9789387669253
- Mahatma Gandhi by Romain Rolland, ISBN: 9789354994722

**Develop your reading habit** | **Gift books to your friends**

# HARDCOVER NON-FICTION

- Meditation and Its Methods by Swami Vivekananda, ISBN: 9789389157987
- Meditations by Marcus Aurelius, ISBN: 9789388118781
- Mein Kampf by Adolf Hitler, ISBN: 9789387669260
- Memory by William Walker Atkinson, ISBN: 9789354990069
- My Inventions: An Autobiography by Nikola Tesla, ISBN: 9789388118187
- My Life : Albert Einstein by GP Editors, ISBN: 9789389157901
- My Life : Dilip Kumar by GP Editors, ISBN: 9789389157994
- Nationalism by Rabindranath Tagore, ISBN: 9789354992025
- State and Revolution by Vladimir Ilich Lenin, ISBN: 9789354990113
- Stolen Legacy by George J.M. James, ISBN: 9789354994753
- Success Through a Positive Mental Attitude by N. Hill, ISBN: 9789390492909
- Tao Te Ching by Lao Tzu, ISBN: 9789354992629
- The Alchemy of Happiness by Al-Ghazzali, ISBN: 9789388118309
- The Art of Living by Epictetus, ISBN: 9789389440539
- The Art of Public Speaking by Dale Carnegie, ISBN: 9789388118477
- The Autobio. of a Yogi by Paramahansa Yogananda, ISBN: 9789387669192
- The Autobiography of Benjamin Franklin, ISBN: 9789389440003
- The Complete Prophecies of Nostradamus, ISBN: 9789354994432
- The Dynamic Laws of Prosperity by Catherine Ponder, ISBN: 9789388118194
- The Elements of Style by William Strunk, ISBN: 9789389157222
- The Federalist Papers by Alexander Hamilton, ISBN: 9789354992841
- The Interpretation of Dreams by Sigmund Freud, ISBN: 9789354992926
- The Kybalion: Philo. of Egypt & Greece by Three Initiates, ISBN: 9789354994845
- The Law and the Promise by Neville Goddard, ISBN: 9789354994852
- The Light of Asia by Sir Edwin Arnold, ISBN: 9789387669130

# HARDCOVER NON-FICTION

- The Miracles of Your Mind by Joseph Murphy, ISBN: 9789387669215
- The Path of Prosperity by James Allen, ISBN: 9789388118323
- The Power of Awareness by Neville Goddard, ISBN: 9789388118330
- The Power of Concentration by Theron Q. Dumont, ISBN: 9789388118224
- The Problem of Increasing Human Energy by Nikola Tesla, ISBN: 9789354990182
- The Problems of Philosophy by Bertrand Russell, ISBN: 9789354994500
- The Quick & Easy Way to Effec. Speaking by Dale Carnegie, ISBN: 9789388118347
- The Science of Being Great by Wallace D. Wattles, ISBN: 9789389440249
- The Science of Being Well by Wallace D. Wattles, ISBN: 9789389440256
- The Science of Mind by Ernest Holmes, ISBN: 9789354990809
- The Secret of Imagining by Neville Goddard, ISBN: 9789389440041
- The Seven Laws of Teaching by John Milton Gregory, ISBN: 9789388118460
- The Story of My Life by Helen Keller, ISBN: 9789389157956
- The Success System that Never Fails by W.C. Stone, ISBN: 9789389440058
- The Ultimate Guide To Success by Julia Seton, ISBN: 9789354993947
- The Wit and Wisdom of Gandhi by Mahatma Gandhi, ISBN: 9789389440560
- The Yoga Sutras of Patanjali by Patanjali, ISBN: 9789389157963
- Think and Grow Rich by Napoleon Hill, ISBN: 9789387669352
- Thoughts are Things by Prentice Mulford, ISBN: 9789354994562
- Up From Slavery by Booker T. Washington, ISBN: 9789389440270
- Value, Price, and Profit by Karl Marx, ISBN: 9789389440065
- Wake Up and Live by Dorothea Brande, ISBN: 9789388118255
- Who were the Shudras by Dr. B.R. Ambedkar, ISBN: 9789354990243
- You Can by George Matthew Adams, ISBN: 9789354995606
- Your Faith is Your Fortune by Neville Goddard, ISBN: 9789389157260

**Develop your reading habit | Gift books to your friends**